पुरातत्त्व

PURĀTATTVA

Bulletin of the Indian Archaeological Society

No. 5 1971-72

Proceedings of the Seminar on OCP & NBP

Editor

S.P. Gupta

Assistant Editors

P.C. Pant

K.N. Dikshit

B.M. Pande

D.K. Printworld (P) Ltd.

New Delhi

Cataloging in Publication Data — DK
[Courtesy : D.K. Agencies (P) Ltd. <docinfo@dkagencies.com>]

Purātattva : bulletin of the Indian Archaeological
Society, no. 5, 1971-72 : proceedings of the
seminar on OCP & NBP / editor, S.P. Gupta ;
assistant editors, P.C. Pant, K.N. Dikshit, B.M.
Pande.

p. cm.
Includes bibliographical references.
ISBN 8124602816

1. Archaeology — India — Periodicals — Congresses.
2. India — Antiquities — Periodicals — Congresses. 3.
India — Civilization — Periodicals — Congresses.
I. Gupta, S.P. II. Indian Archaeological Society.

First Reprinted in 2005
ISBN 81-246-0281-6
Price for volume 5 (1971-72): Rs. 600 US $ 30

Reprint authorised by
Indian Archaeological Society
New Delhi - 110 016

Purātattva is published annually.
Manuscripts (whether in the form of articles or notes or book reviews) offered for publication should be sent to the Editor, Purātattva, Indian Archaeological Society, B-17, Qutab Institutional Area, New Delhi - 110 016.

Published and printed by:
D.K. Printworld (P) Ltd.
'Srikunj,' F-52, Bali Nagar
New Delhi – 110015
Phone : (011) 2545 3975, 2546 6019 Fax : (011) 2546 5926
E-mail : dkprintworld@vsnl.net
www. dkprintworld.com

CONTENTS

Editorial

No. 5 of the Bulletin is before you. It has been devoted primarily to the proceedings of the Seminar on OCP and NBP convened by Shri K. N. Dikshit and held in May 1971 in the National Museum, New Delhi. Although the first draft was prepared by me, I, due to my heavy preoccupation with the printing of my book *Disposal of the Dead and Physical Types in Ancient India*, was unable to revise it and prepare it for the press. I, therefore, requested my senior colleague Dr. Y. D. Sharma to finalize the draft, get some of the the illustrations drawn in his office and prepare the bibliographies. I gratefully acknowledge his most willing help into the matter.

Fortunately, Shri B. K. Thapar, our General Secretary, is now with us once again after his return from Cambridge. We are happy to include his note also. We gratefully acknowledge the greetings from our former General Secretary, Dr. A. K. Narain, now Visiting Professor in the Wisconsian University. I, however, regret to record a wrong information printed in the editorial of the last number of the Bulletin and brought to my notice by my friend Shri I. K. Sharma : Shri V. D. Krishnaswami died in a hospital at Banglore and not Hyderabad.

During the last decade archaeological activities in India were concentrated not only in western India but also in Punjab, Harayana and western U.P. The so called Dark Age—between the later days of the Harappa culture and the beginning of the Painted Grey Ware period—was slowly and gradually getting lighted. However, due to the prolific writings of Prof. Sankalia, including his excavation reports of Navdatoli, etc., only the chalcolithic cultures of western India and the Deccan became known to the students and teachers in the universities of India and abroad ; the knowledge of the Copper Age cultures of the Punjab and Harayana remained confined to the field archaeologists. The present seminar-proceedings seek to remove this lop-sided emphasis on the chalcolithic cultures of western India by bringing into light the personality of the OCP culture and the crucial role that is played in bringing the Harappa culture into contact with the Copper Hoards of the Ganga basin. In the second millennium B. C. it served as a great bridge between Punjab and Uttar Pradesh. In socio-cultural terms it seems to have sustained and carried forward the 'system' that was created by the Preharappans and maintained by the Harappans. Some of the religio-cultural elements of the present day Hinduism, now identified as Harappan in origin, certainly passed through the OCP, PGW and NBP complexes. This is what Malik calls 'continuation' of 'Indian style' through the process of 'Indinization' in his monograph *Indian Civilization : Formative Period*, reviewed in the last number of the Bulletin. Here, some glimpse of that process can be had through the Ochre Coloured Pottery complex.

It may be emphasized that at least one more seminar of this nature is essential. The theme should be something like this: Archaeology of the second millinnium B.C. in and around Punjab and Haryana. Broadly speaking, it should bring out in relief the interplay of cultural forms that the Preharappan and Harappan complexes were assuming due to various internal and external factors in the period between the later days of the Harappans and the beginning of the PGW. In this context appendices on Siswal, Mitathal, Bara and Bahedrabad are extremely significant. How I wish there is one more Sankalia with us in India to write the archaeology of Punjab and Haryana of the second millinnium B. C.

S. P. Gupta

GENERAL SECRETARY'S NOTE

One of the principal aims and objects of the Indian Archaeological Society is 'to hold periodical seminars and gatherings for academic purposes.' With a view to fulfilling this task worthily, the Society organised, in May 1971, a seminar on Ochre Colour and Northern Black Polished Wares, of which the proceedings are published in the present issue of *Puratattva*. Apart from reporting the discussions in the sessions on these two Wares, opportunity has also been taken to include, under appendices, other relevant material, which provides a perspective to the problems discussed.

The value of such seminars in archaeological investigations does not need any elucidation here. Suffice it to mention that they provide an occasion, through informed criticism, for the proper evaluation of the available evidence. In the present case, the evidence on these two ceramic industries had been accumulating during the last two decades, and, in the words of Sir Mortimer Wheeler, had taken the shape of an 'untidy heap'. It was felt desirable, therefore, that this 'heap' should be given 'an assured place in the landscape' of Indian archaeology.

The various issues related to these ceramic industries have been discussed in sufficient detail with patient objectiveness. As I was not present at the time of this seminar, I would like to bring to the notice of the scholars some of the problems, notably concerning the 'Copper Hoards', which have remained an unsolved mystery. Why were the 'Copper Hoards' found localized at one place on a site? Is the deposition of the copper objects in hoards a normal feature in the life of the community? If so, does the findspot represent the armoury of the community or the workshop of the guild of smiths? At Saipai, where the excavation has been conducted with an informed purpose, the harpoon and the hooked-sword (obtained from the excavation proper) were found at varying depths below surface (respectively 45 and 28 cm.), within a radius of five metres of the reported find of the 'Hoard' (at about 30 cm. below surface). Pottery continued to occur to a depth of 91 cm., with a concentration between 8 and 51 cm. Does this phenomenon prove or disprove the hypothesis of sheet-flooding in this area? Arising from this is the problem of the composition of the Copper Hoard- and pottery-bearing deposit. Although this aspect of enquiry concerns largely the sedimentologist, to the naked-eye there does not seem to be any appreciable difference between the composition of the soil containing the 'Copper Hoards' and the pottery, and the natural soil, underneath it or, for that matter, even the deposit lying against the so-called settlement (as observed at Saipai, and Nasirpur) We may also consider the functional aspect of the objects and study their use-marks, if any. It has been pointed out elsewhere that 'this tool-kit has a predominant hunting bias', but the evidence seems to be more indicative than conclusive. From the nature and contents of the various 'Hoards' it is apparent that they did not belong to an individual family but were intended to be used for a specified purpose by the community as a whole or at least by a section of it. This would imply the organization of the society into different sections, some of which might have been practising husbandry. The occurrence of stone pestles and rubbers at Saipai, Lal Qila and Ambkheri already suggests the use of cereals. In fact, the economic base of the Copper Hoard Culture still remains to be properly investigated.

B. K. Thapar

Erratum : The press regrets a misprint on page 4. Second sentence of para one should read : Short articles, etc., on Bahadrabad, Baharia, Noh and Saipai, have been added . . .

OCP AND NBP : 1971

Proceedings of the Seminar held by the Indian Archaeological Society, on the 11th May, 1971, at the National Museum, New Delhi, on Ochre-Coloured Ware and Northern Black Polished Ware

Edited by
Dr. Y. D. Sharma

SOME RECOMMENDATIONS

1. That the term OCP should be retained for the present.

2. However, when in full it may be written with small letters (ochre-colour pottery or ware), indicating the particular variety by site name in bracket, e.g., OCP (Bahadrabad).

3. The term NBP should be retained.

SEMINAR ON OCP AND NBP WARES

Inaugurated by	Shri C. Sivaramamurti
General President	Shri A. Ghosh
General Secretary	Dr. S. P. Gupta
Convener	Shri K. N. Dikshit

SESSION ON OCP

Chairman	Shri M. N. Deshpande
Secretary	Shri K. N. Dikshit

SESSION ON NBP

Chairman	Dr. K. K. Sinha
Secretary	Dr. D. P. Agrawal

OTHER PARTICIPANTS

1.	Shri Amrendra Nath	New Delhi
2.	Shri B. K. Bhattacharya	New Delhi
3.	Shri B. M. Pandey	-do-
4.	Shri B. N. Tandon	-do-
5.	Miss Chhaya Bhattacharya	-do-
6	Shri J. G. Mathur	Nagpur
7.	Shri J. S. Nigam	New Delhi
8.	Shri K. C. Verma	Ghaziabad
9.	Shri K. Deva	New Delhi
10.	Shri K. S. Ramachandran	-do-
11.	Shri L. M. Wahal	Kanpur
12.	Dr. L. Morton Smith	Toronto, Canada
13	Shri M. C. Joshi	New Delhi
14.	Miss M. Donavan	-do-
15.	Shri B. L. Nagarch	Bhopal
16.	Shri N. C. Ghosh	New Delhi
17.	Dr. N. R. Banerjee	Kathmandu, Nepal
18.	Dr. (Mrs.) Omi Manchanda	New Delhi
19.	Shri R. C. Gaur	Aligarh
20.	Shri R. G. Pandey	Calcutta
21.	Shri R. P. Sharma	New Delhi
22.	Dr. R. S. Mittal	Roorkee
23.	Dr. Romila Thapar	New Delhi
24.	Shri Shankar Nath	New Delhi
25.	Shri Suraj Bhan	Kurukshetra
26.	Shri W. H. Siddiqi	New Delhi
27.	Dr. Y. D. Sharma	-do-

FOREWORD

In its last annual general meeting held at Nagpur in November, 1970, the Indian Archaeological Society decided to organise group discussions on the Ochre-Coloured Pottery (OCP) and the Northern Black Polished Ware (NBP), with a view to settle certain issues posed by recent field researches. The issues related to nomenclature, date, culture-contacts and diffusion of these two wares.

Accordingly, a day-long seminar was arranged on the 11th May, 1971. Through the hospitality of the authorities of the National Museum, the seminar took place in the Committee Room of the National Museum, New Delhi.

All scholars who had reported on either of the two wares named above, as a result of field-work carried out by them, were invited to participate in the seminar and also to bring some specimens of the wares for a fruitful discussion.

Altogether, thirty-five scholars attended the seminar at the invitation of Shri K. N. Dikshit, the convener. Shri A. Ghosh, former Director General of the Archaeological Survey of India, took the chair as the General President, while Shri M. N. Deshpande and Dr. K. K. Sinha acted as Chairmen respectively for the sessions on the OCP and NBP. Dr. S. P. Gupta, the moving force behind the seminar, was the General Secretary while Shri K. N. Dikshit and Dr. D. P. Agrawal were the Sectional Secretaries of the OCP and NBP sessions respectively. Shri C. Sivaramamurti, Director, National Museum, inaugurated the seminar.

The session on the OCP decided that in view of the differences on the issues involved, it was not possible to settle them at this stage. A helpful procedure would, therefore, be to publish drawings of selected pottery from different so-called OCP sites, together with a brief note on ancillary findings, and to place this publication before the next annual general meeting of the Society for such action as it may decide to take in future.

We have not found it possible to act exactly in accordance with the above decision. But along with the proceedings of the seminar, we have included drawings of selected pottery from important OCP and allied sites, in order to enable the next general meeting of the Society to take suitable further action.

The speeches and comments as supplied by different speakers, or as very kindly recorded by Sarvashri Ram Swarup and O. D. Dogra of the Archaeological Survey of India, New Delhi, are being reported here with the minimum of pruning and recasting, mainly in order to avoid repetitions and superficialities. It is hoped that this publication would encourage further deliberations, leading ultimately to a satisfactory solution of the issues involved. The seminar provided on opportunity to scholars and field-workers to meet and exchange views. It is left to the readers to decide what success attended the brief seminar. We, on our part, are most grateful to the participants who spared a full day from their busy life to attend it.

A bibliography of important articles have been included in the appendices. Short on Bahadrabad, Baharia, Noh and Saipai, articles etc. have been added, also as appendices, to make the proceedings a self-contained compendium on the subjects discussed. We have also included extracts from scientific reports on the NBP.

We acknowledge with thanks the loan of a few blocks of line-drawings of potteries given by the Director General of Archaeology in India. Similarly, we thank Prof. G. R. Sharma of the University of Allahabad for sending us the so far unpublished material of his excavations at Baharia, and Shri B. B. Lal and Shri L. M. Wahal for the drawings of pottery from Saipai, their epoch-making discovery. Our grateful thanks are due to many colleagues in the Archaeological Survey of India, New Delhi, particularly to Sarvashri A. K. Ghosh, M. S. Mani and S. S. Saar for the excellent drawings and to Shri Gulshan Lal for typing the manuscript.

★

INAUGURAL SPEECH BY C. SIVARAMAMURTI

The Indian Archaeology Society is again holding a seminar, and this time at New Delhi. We have amidst us today, Shri A. Ghosh, occupying the chair as the General President of the seminar. We should be proud of this moment, and we are grateful to him for his presence here. Today, if Indian archaeology is understood widely, it is largely due to him. We know that archaeology, in all its aspects, is dear to him. Shri Ghosh combines the past and the present. The Indian Archaeological Society should be proud of holding this seminar under the presidentship of Shri Ghosh, who would guide the deliberations today. In welcoming Shri Ghosh to the National Museum, which is his old haunt, we are very grateful to him and accord him a hearty welcome. I am also sure, you will all make this seminar a great success.

INTRODUCTION

by A. Ghosh

Shri Sivaramamurti has praised me, although I do not know how much I deserve his praise. Anyway, I appreciate the sentiments expressed by him. The subject of discussion today is the OCP and NBP wares. While the subjects have been discussed on many an occasion before, and there are many publications dealing with them, I do hope that the deliberations of this seminar will throw some new light on the problems, particularly those that Dr. D. P. Agrawal has on C^{14} dating, I request Shri Deshpande now to speak and open the session on the OCP.

SESSION ON OCP

M. N. Deshpande (Chairman)

The OCP has been a subject of discussion, and it continues to be so in spite of the work of the last twenty years. You may remember that shri Lal's efforts at Hastinapura brought to light in the lower levels a ware, which he described as Ochre-coloured Ware (Lal, 1954-55). He himself has not been very happy about the designation of this ware (fig. 5) for he found this ware, which was probably ill-fired and not slipped, when rubbed, assumed a different shape. Moreover, while writing the report, he was faced with the problem of placing it in definite cultural context. He thought perhaps it would be associated with the Copper Hoards of the Ganga valley, and extended in region of Bihar and beyond the Vindhyas. In order to pursue the problem further, he made some digging at Bisauli and Rajpur Parsu (Lal, 1951) and here also he found pottery which was designated by him as OCP. Subsequently, Y. D. Sharma did some excavation at Bahadrabad (Sharma, 1961). At one place of the site, some digging was going on for the sake of a canal, and the canal-diggers had found some red pottery and copper implements. It was after this that Sharma excavated this very area, and got the same pottery which could be called OCP. Unfortunately, no copper tool was found by him.

For my part, I explored the upper Gangetic valley with students of the School of Archaeology and encountered a number of OCP sites. Of these, Ambkheri interested me most although the mound there was not very prominent. Again, close by, there was another site named Gadharona, about 6 kms. north of Ambkheri. Further south, we examined the site at Nasirpur where I was told that a copper hoard had been found earlier and now it is exhibited in the Gurukul Kangri Museum, near Hardwar. As a result of this exploration, a small-scale excavation was carried out at Ambkheri (Deshpande, 1965-1 and 1967-1). Shri K. N. Dikshit actively assisted me in this work. The occupational deposit of the OCP here varied from 1·00 to 1·25m. We did not get a single sherd with any painting. The slip has a tendency to peel off. For the first time we got a variety of OCP shapes, not noticed before in any excavation. Noteworthy types included large trough, bowl-like lid with central knob, dish-on-stand with drooping rim, vase with horizontally splayed out rim, ring-stand and basin with under-cut rim (fig. 2). Associated with this pottery was a washed grey ware. Other associated finds include : a carnelian bead, terracotta objects like cart-wheel, animal figures (humped bull), and a fragmentary cake, and stone objects. Remains of a brick-kiln and a hearth were also noticed. I also excavated another site called Bargaon, situated on the right bank of river Maskara, a tributary of the Yamuna (Deshpande, 1967-2), where we got a very fine chert blade, a copper bangle (also a fragmentary chisel in exploration) and painted pottery of definite Harappan variety (figs. 3, 4). We also found some pots where the slip peeled off like the OCP.

Subsequently, two more sites were taken up for excavations: Lal-Qila and Saipai. The latter site was excavated by Shri B. B. Lal and L. M. Wahal of the Archaeological Survey where Copper Hoard tools were encountered for the first time with the OCP. (see Comments by Shri Wahal *p. 10 -ed.*).

In the course of further explorations, a large number of OCP sites have come to light from eastern Punjab (Dikshit, 1967-1), western U. P. and eastern Rajasthan. Evidently the OCP area is quite extensive (fig. 1).

Some scholars have also given thought to the nature of this pottery. This could be due to water-logging as a result of deluge (Lal, 1968). However, on the basis of the analysis of the soil samples from Atranjikhera and other sites, Dr. B. B. Lal thinks otherwise (Dr. Lal, 1969). He does not agree that the ware was water-logged for a long time. However, I must point out that even at Ambkheri, the layers were not very distinctive, although we found hand-made bricks of different sizes, as also ash in the OCP horizon. At Jhinjhana in Muzaffarnagar district (Rishi, 1965), the random distribution of the sherds was noticed in the section.

Now I come to the problem whether it is necessary to change the term OCP. Everybody has expressed dissatisfaction with the present nomenclature. But if we change it now, there might arise some confusion. The second point is : Can we definitely establish the identity of this ware with the Copper Hoards ? If it is so, what is the nature of associated pottery of Copper Hoards in Bihar ? This problem has also to be tackled. Lohuizen connected a copper object found at Lothal with the anthropomorphic figure of the Copper Hoard (Lohuizen, 1960). We may have to consider OCP's relationship with the Harappans also. Did it have an independent origin (Dikshit, 1970 and Gupta, 1963)? Is it confined to the central Ganga-Yamuna Doab? From where did it originate? What about the Modhera (in District Mehsana, Gujarat) Copper Hoard reported by S. P. Gupta ? Can we relate all these tools and sites ? Why in most of the OCP sites clear stratification is absent ? How does the character of the pottery differ in the upper, central and lower Ganga-Yamuna Doab ?

I hope, the participants would touch upon all these problems while making their comments and offering suggestions.

S. P. Gupta

As far back as 1964, in the All-India seminar on Indian Prehistory held at Poona, I had put forward a few of my views on the OCP, which I would like to reiterate here with additional reasons. As we all know, the credit of recognizing this ware as a separate entity in the entire gamut of ancient Indian potteries goes solely to B.B. Lal (Lal, 1947; 1954-55). I would like to emphasise the words *separate entity*, because Lal could not see in the OCP an admixture of the Harappan pottery. I would again like to emphasize the words *could not*, because Lal had taken a particular stand on the problem of the Copper Hoards vis-a-vis the OCP. According to him, in the Ganga-Yamuna Doab the Copper Hoards and the OCP go hand in hand but the Copper Hoard tools and the Harappan tools have nothing in common. Obviously, if the Copper Hoard tools were different from the Harappan tools, how could the potteries associated with them be the same? But then some of the excavations in the upper Doab, particularly at Bahadrabad and Ambkheri, created some problems; since, although, by and large, the pottery at these sites looked like the OCP, it contained unmistakable elements of the Harappan ware, particularly in the typology of vases and basins, and also, probably, dish-on-stand. Obviously, in the Poona seminar some of the participants felt that the OCP had no independent status of its own; one of them called it only a late Harappan ware. Somehow, I could not subscribe to any of these views. I felt that the evidence was not enough to dislodge the OCP from its independent pedestal. I agreed with Lal that in the Ganga-Yamuna Doab the OCP was associated with the Copper Hoards. This has now been proved by the excavations at Saipai, district Etawah, by L. M. Wahal. Obviously, the epicentre of this ware has to be sought in the area of greatest concentration of the Copper Hoards (Gupta, 1965). This area, on our present knowing, falls between Etah and Kanpur and includes the districts of Fatehgarh and Etawah. Since in one of my papers on Copper Hoards (Gupta, 1963). I had visualised the movement of the Copper Hoard people from the east to the west and of the Harappans from the west to the east, it was easy for me to visualise their contact in the upper Doab sites giving rise to the hybrid nature of the pottery at sites like Ambkheri. It means that as we go west of Bithur in district Kanpur, situated in lower Doab, we are likely to get more and more the admixture of the Harappan ware in the pottery complex of the OCP sites.

My analysis of the entire situation, therefore, brings out four facts: firstly, the Copper Hoard people were the late contemporaries of the Harappans; secondly, the OCP people came in contact with the Harappans in the upper Doab; thirdly, the OCP has a separate entity, and, finally, the epicentre of the OCP lies between Etah and Kanpur, although its origin seems to lie somewhere between Etawah and Kanpur.

I, therefore, plead for retaining the term OCP for a ware which was essentially non-Harappan to begin with, but which, in a particular culture-contact situation in the upper Doab, imbibed a number of Harappan traits. I am not inclined to call it pre-Harappan, since on circumstantial evidence (Gupta, 1963) I do not date the Copper Hoards prior to 2000 B.C. I also do not consider it as totally post-Harappan, since at one stage, probably between 1800 B.C. and 1600 B.C., it overlapped with the Harappan pottery. I am inclined to consider it as a late contemporary of the Harappan ware, which continued to flourish in post-Harappan times. Although stratigraphically it has so far not been found overlapping at the upper end with the Painted Grey Ware, such a possibility cannot be completely ruled out, particularly, in Haryana and western U.P. The Modhera hoard has four antennae swords of bronze which will soon be published.

K. N. Dikshit

The present nomenclature of the ware, to my mind, should be retained. The study of the OCP from different sites reveals two areas of development : (a) central Doab, and (b) upper Doab and east Punjab. These two areas are distinguished entirely on the basis of the comparative ceramic types present and absent in the Harappan complex of this region. The pottery types in area (a) are not only limited, but their finish is also inferior, whereas the area (b) has a variety of utilitarian types, also present in the Harappan complex (including Bara) of this region (Dikshit, 1970).

The jar with horizontally splayed out rim is a common type of the areas (a) and (b) and late Harappan. The typical compartmented incised designs noticed in area (a) have a close resemblance with similar patterns at Bara (Dikshit, 1969-1).

The complete absence of the Harappan traits from most of the OCP sites of area (b) shows that the OCP in that area had nothing to do with the Harappans.

The users of the OCP were the original inhabitants of the Ganga valley and their migrational trend was from the central Ganga-Yamuna Doab(Baharia, district Shahjahanpur, U.P.) to upper Ganga-Yamuna Doab and east Punjab (Katpalon, district Jullundur, Punjab).

As the soil analysis of the OCP strata is still under the active consideration of sedimentologists, it is difficult for archaeologists to accept or discard any view (flood or wind-blown action) regarding the mode of transportation and deposition of the material in which pottery etc. are found buried. (For the controversy, see Dr. B.B. Lal, Shri B.B. Lal, and others elsewhere in the volume, -*ed.*).

D. P. Agrawal

The problem of OCP has defied all solution, because we have not made a systematic multi-pronged attack on it so far.

There are various confusing issues :

(i) Dr. B. B. Lal has tried to prove that OCP-associated deposits are aeolean in origin (Dr. Lal, 1969). How can one then explain the interspersing of potsherds in these deposits? The confusion gets worse confounded by Shri B. B. Lal's use of the same data for proving fluviatile nature of the sediments (Lal, 1968).

(ii) There are various pottery affinities suggested: from Harappan, Cemetery-H to Bara.

(iii) At Saipai, an association of the OCP and Copper Hoards is reported. But have we one uniform OCP in the whole of Doab, or are there a number of OCPs ?

(iv) What is the definition of OCP repertoire?

So long as one keeps on arguing on a subjective basis, there cannot be any meaningful solution of these problems. The first step, therefore, should be to collect more data in a systematic way. I, therefore, suggest the following plan of action:

(a) Leading workers, like Lal, Deshpande, Gaur, Sharma, Wahal, Dikshit and Suraj Bhan, should be asked to report on the OCP shapes of their sites.

(b) Under the leadership of the Society, a comparative morphology should be compiled.

(c) Sedimentological analyses from a number of sites be carried out to determine the origin of the sterile sediments associated with the OCP.

(d) Metallurgical analyses of a large number of Copper Hoard artefacts should be carried out to determine the techniques used, as also to correlate them to the mines exploited.

(e) These multiple data should be published for scholars to synthesise them for resolving the problem of the OCP.

If the above steps are taken expeditiously, we will soon be able to say something meaningful and tangible about the OCP.

R. C. Gaur

On the basis of a few pottery types the OCP was taken by some scholars as a handiwork of the Harappan refugees (Ghosh and others, 1965). The degenerate state of pottery has been attributed to long-time water-logging. However, a detailed study of the pottery types and the habitational pattern of the OCP people and those of the Harappans has shown that the material cultures of the two peoples are different from each other, and independent. The presence of a few Harappan pottery shapes at Bahadrabad (Sharma, 1961), and Ambkheri (Deshpande; 1965; 1967-1) merely suggests that the two cultures had flourished simultaneously at least for some time, and their peoples had come in close contact with each other somewhere near the western border of Uttar Pradesh, and both had borrowed something from each other.

However, the sites which are away from the border were almost free from the Harappan influence and their deposits bear local and indigenous features. Of all these sites, two, viz., Atranjikhera and Lal-Qila, are typical and important. Both of these have many common features and may broadly be grouped together. Both the sites have yielded painted as well as incised pottery in considerable number (figs. 6 and 7). These devices for decorating pottery are conspicuous by their absence at other OCP sites. However, Saipai, which is also an easterly site, has yielded pottery with incised designs (see article in appendices, *-ed.*). The majority of the shapes at these three sites are common, and, therefore, they maintain regional homogeneity. While much is known now about the OCP of Atranjikhera (Gaur, 1965-1, 2; 1969), the detailed report on Saipai is awaited. It would, therefore, be better if we analyse here briefly the chief characteristics of the Lal-Qila pottery.

The general features usually noted about the OCP at other sites, viz. rolled edges, porous, powdery surface, ill-firing, etc. are rare at Lal-Qila. This major difference may be due to the fact that Lal-Qila pottery complex comes from an undisturbed habitational site, whereas the other complexes belong to disturbed sites, presumably, al affected by water-logging or other weathering conditions.

Lal-Qila pottery deposit includes a variety of shapes (fig. 7), which may be classified broadly into seven groups : 1. storage jars; 2. vases; 3. basins; 4. bowls; 5. lids; 6. dishes-on-stand (?); and 7. miniature pots. Among these shapes, vases represent the richest variety of types, including those which have vertical handles attached between the rim and the shoulder (no. 4). Basins and bowls are available in different sizes and are generally deep. One of the bowls (no. 9) indicates that a set of legs was attached to it at the base, while a few of the big basins had horizontally or vertically attached looped handles (nos. 5, 12). It may be noted that while a large number of handles were found at Atranjikhera, complete pots with handles were not found. However pots with ring base is a common feature at Atranjikhera. Though not a single complete dish-on-stand has been found, broken sherds indicate that some type of dish-on-stand is also present at Lal-Qila. The excavation has yielded a variety of interesting miniature pots, generally complete.

Atranjikhera was the first site to have yielded painted designs on the OCP, but Lal-Qila pottery has considerably increased our knowledge about their technique and motifs. These appear to have been executed with bold hand. Among the interesting paintings mention may be made of an elongated humped bull, segregated leafy design, floral motif, hatched triangles, circles, etc.

As compared to Atranjikhera, though the incised designs here are fewer in number, their lines are deeper and larger. A significant discovery was the graffiti marks noticed for the first time on OCP sherds. Typical ochrous sherds are small in number at Lal-Qila, since they come from proper habitational layers.

J. S. Nigam

To my mind, the term OCP needs change. I have classified the OCP sites and have divided them into four groups. In the first group are sites like Ambkheri, Hastinapura and Noh, where no copper has been found. In the second group are sites which yield OCP along with copper tools. These are, Bahadrabad, Bargaon and Saipai. The third group includes sites where OCP has not been found, although copper tools are reported with other wares. The fourth group includes sites where only copper tools have been found, and no other find is reported.

The OCP has red ochrous, yellow ochrous and greyish pottery. I also recall that the Harappan wares are of corresponding three colours, i.e., red, buff and grey. I feel that the ware in different regions is outwardly similar but there are variations in fabric, and as such the OCP of a particular type may be named after type site, such as Bahadrabad ware, Atranjikhera ware, and the like.

L. M. Wahal

Saipai, a village in tehsil and district Etawah, is situated about 18 km. north from Etawah Railway Station and is connected by road which leads to Mainpuri. It is a small village with a predominant population of cultivators.

In July, 1969, while ploughing a field, a Copper Hoard was reported from the village and most of the implements were carried away by the police for investigation. Only a few implements out of the big hoard, were returned to the owner of the land. These were later sold by the owner to a local hawker who melted them for disposal as molten metal.

Shortly after the report of the hoard came to my notice, I rushed to the site and investigated the matter further and after a great deal of persuasion, I could obtain from the dealer only one hooked sword, which was later shown by me to Shri B.B. Lal. Keeping in view the importance of the hoard and the site, a trial sounding was initiated by me, which was, later on, extended under the instructions of Shri Lal. During the operations, one hooked sword and one harpoon were found along with ochre-coloured ware. It firmly established the missing link between the typical copper hoard tools and OCP. Since the association of the hoard with the OCP has been established here, I humbly suggest that instead of calling it OCP culture. it may be called Copper Hoard Culture.

The land at Saipai is flat, covering an area of about two *bighas* with a deposit of 1·00 to 1·15 m. The occurrence of a small Harappan type chert blade during the excavation needs further investigation. The nature of the ware, as is evident from its name, runs from orange to red colour, and in a few cases it retains a slip. Mostly, vases, bowls and basins were found. The rims of these vessels were splayed out, flaring, incurved or outcurved. Dish-on-stand is suspected. There are several pots with strap handles, as also pots with short but pronounced spouts and lips. (see article in appendices, *-ed.*)

The excavated deposit at this site also, by and large, was devoid of prominently marked regular layers of habitational debris. But I could not detect any disturbance in the layers; the deposits were simply mixed. I myself cannot assert whether the site was subjected to any flood or not but the slip on most of the pots has peeled off and the overall nature of the pottery indicates water-weathering.

M. C. Joshi

The Copper Hoard implements of western U. P. sites should be associated with OCP or other red wares with great caution, particularly in view of the highly refined cast tools, indicating complicated copper technology. In the light of such tools, the standard of economy reflected in excavated material from the sites appears to be very poor, indicating semi-hunting pastoral economy. How could the people, who prepared such fine implements, have such an ordinary culture? I, therefore, feel that either these tools have no connection with the OCP or similar other cultures, or else they belong to an earlier Copper-Bronze Age culture.

N. C. Ghosh

In my view till the association of the Copper Hoards and the OCP is firmly established at more than one site, the pottery (OCP) should be termed as Bahadrabad Ware. The types from Bahadrabad should form a key to further classification tor upper Doab. There are certain types which are common between Ahichchhatra and Bahadrabad. (see article in appendices, -ed.)

I have also observed that a number of painted pots, particularly of Bara fabric, tend to appear like OCP owing to weathering after excavation, unless chemically treated and preserved immediatly on exposure. Therefore, there exist many chances of wrong identification, if we simply go by colour scheme and do not give due regard to typology.

I would plead for a comparative study of the Bahadrabad pottery. (See article in the appendices *-ed.*)

Shankar Nath

The pottery called OCP was first christened at Hastinapura, on the basis of the fabric and texture of the ceramic. This name was not given in any cultural context at that time. Some of the OCP sites explored in recent years have produced pottery shapes comparable with Harappan, whereas a number of sites also show local characteristics. It is not yet certain as to who the people responsible for the manufacture of this particular kind of ceramic were. Whether they were the Harappans or some separate group of people inhabiting the Ganga-Yamuna Doab? Till this problem is finally settled, I feel that we should retain the nomenclature, because OCP is the name given to a particular kind of pottery and not to any culture.

This pottery is accompanied by a grey ware which also has all the characteristics of OCP. However, at present the whole lot is called as OCP, and I differ with the suggestion of J. S. Nigam that as OCP complex has also got some percentage of grey ware sherds, its nomenclature should be changed.

I have myself explored at least two dozen sites of this ware in district Saharanpur, while doing village-to-village survey. On the basis of my experience, I would like to emphasise that none of the sites is extensive, not being more than 100 m. on each side. The occupational deposit ranges between 0·75 to 1·50 m. The types are limited, as pottery from Anwarpur Baroli shows (fig. 12). What does this indicate? Perhaps it is indicative of a short span of time for the habitation at one place. Saharanpur district is the region in upper Doab where Harappan and OCP sherds have been picked up from the same site.

Most of the OCP sites are considered to be devoid of structural remains, except a hearth and brick-kiln, noticed at Ambkheri, where traces of hand-made bricks were found (Deshpande, 1967-1). A wedge-shaped burnt brick was also noticed in explorations at Hardakheri, and as the site is a pure OCP one, this brick fulfils all conditions for being called an ochre-coloured brick.

Almost all the OCP sites have yielded ill-fired pottery. Does this imply that the ceramic was deliberately ill-fired and ill-firing was not accidental? Or, does it mean that the people who fashioned this pottery were not competent enough or expert in preparing ceramic of quality? The question needs proper investigation.

There are a number of sites which are below the present ground surface and pottery was collected from pits dug by the villagers. Most probably these underground sites were situated at comparatively low levels and were covered by deposits either brought by floods or winds during the passage of time.

N. R. Banerjee

I should like to agree with D.P. Agrawal. We should be definite in our minds if copper tools are associated with OCP.

Everybody knows that water rises due to earth-movements and earthquakes. In Nepal, where Asoka had gone and where there are monuments associated with Buddha, I find a lot of pottery, grey and NBP wares included, without any slip. Such appearance of pottery, which is characteristic of the OCP, could be due to flood.

K. Deva

The OCP deposit at all known sites is shallow, not exceeding 1·5 m. in thickness. From the evidence of the site of Saipai, discovered by L. M. Wahal, no doubt is left regarding the identity of the authors of the OCP and the Copper Hoards. The uniformly shallow deposits indicate that the authors of the OCP were a nomadic people who did not lead a settled life at any site for a considerable time. They perhaps lived in temporary huts or shelters and subsisted partly on hunting and fishing and partly on a mixed pastoral-cum-agricultural economy. As a nomadic people they formed a vagrant culture.

From the variety of sophisticated copper tools found among the Copper Hoards, it is clear that the authors were proficient in smelting copper and fashioned them in a number of sophisticated shapes, like shouldered celt, harpoon, antennae sword and anthropomorph. Their pottery also shows a fair variety of types and frequent use of incised and, in rare cases, even simple painted designs. The fabric is medium to thin and much of the pottery originally was slipped. Owing to these sites being subjected to frequent flooding, the pottery not only lost its slip but also became friable and brittle. This is the result obviously of water-logging and not of indifferent firing or lack of potter's skill. A people who knew the technique of smelting copper at a high temperature certainly should have known how to fire pottery properly.

The anthropomorph is more likely to be a primitive object of magic or cult significance rather than a tool or weapon. The early form of *srivatsa* appears to have been derived from it. I do not agree with D. P. Agrawal that it was a missile or a weapon similar to modern boomerang.

Suraj Bhan

Much water has flown since the discovery at Hastinapura of the ill-preserved, pale red ware, of medium to fine fabric, seemingly wheel-turned and called the Ochre-Coloured Ware or OCP (Lal, 1954-55). The pottery bearing family likeness to Lal's OCP has been reported from nearly 90 sites in the Ganga-Yamuna Doab and from Noh near Bharatpur in Rajasthan. More than half a dozen of these sites have been excavated, including Bahadrabad, Ambkheri, Atranjikhera, Ahichchhatra (Banerjee, 1969), and Saipai, details of which have been given today by L. M. Wahal. These excavations have expanded our horizon on the nature of deposit, the ceramic complexes and the associated finds. The sporadic occurrence of the OCP in yellow brown sandy deposit devoid of any sign of habitation and imperceptibly merging into the natural soil is significant (Lal, 1968). The discovery of a burnt brick at Bahadrabad, an ovaloid oven dug in the ground and lined with hand-made mud bricks at Ambkheri, perhaps used for manufacturing *gur* and another at Ahichchhatra, and a terracotta bull at Ambkheri only emphasise the extreme paucity of antiquities and structural remains in the culture. However, the discovery of the Copper Hoards from Rajpur Parsu, Bisauli, Bahadrabad, Nasirpur and Saipai indicates the richness of the OCP culture in copper implements. The tools include the typical harpoon, anthropomorph, hooked spearhead, flat celt and ring.

Where preserved, the pots show a thick red slip, which is rarely painted with black bands. At Atranjikhera, the incised decoration on the exterior of pots marks a distinct note. The main pottery shapes of OCP, as illustrated by K. Deva and R. C. Gaur (Deva, 1969; Gaur, 1969) include:

1. vase with out-curved rim and ledged neck (Gaur),
2. vase with flaring rim (Deva, no. 1; Gaur),
3. vase with flanged rim (Deva, no. 1b; Gaur),
4. bowl-like lid with a central knob (Deva, no. 14),
5. bowl-with convex profile and blunted rim (Deva, no. 13),
6. bowl with flaring rim (Gaur),
7. bowl with flanged rim (Gaur),
8. bowl with convex profile (Gaur),

9. basin with beaded undercut rim (Deva, no. 22),
10. dish-on-stand with short drooping rim (Deva, no. 9),
11. dish-on-stand with long drooping rim (Deva, no. 8),
12. dish-on-stand with hooked rim (Deva, no. 7c),
13. squat stem of dish-on-stand (Deva, A),
14. loop handle vase (Gaur),
15. channel spout (Gaur),
16. tubular spout (Gaur),
17. ring-footed bowl or vase (Gaur), and
18. flask (Ambkheri, fig. 2 no. 11).

As to the authorship of the OCP there exist mainly two shades of opinion among Indian scholars. The first view expressed by Y. D. Sharma (Sharma, 1961), though later modified and subsequently supported by A. Ghosh and other (Sharma, 1965; Handa, 1968), identified the OCP with a degenerate Harappa culture carried to the Doab by refugees. The recently growing second view that the ware is essentially non-Harappan with only marginal Harappan influences at sites like Ambkheri and showing regional features in incised decorations at Atranjikhera is held by S. P. Gupta, M. N. Deshpande, K. Deva, K N. Dikshit and R. C. Gaur (Gupta, 1963; Deshpande, 1969-1; Deva, 1969; Dikshit, 1969; Gaur, 1970). In the absence of published reports on the excavated OCP sites, one is greatly handicapped in examining the problem with any amount of thoroughness. At least a detailed catalogue of OCP types, so meaningfully suggested by H. D. Sankalia in the annual conference of the Archaeological Society at Nagpur and emphasised by D. P. Agrawal, is an outstanding need to facilitate a serious study of the OCP problem. I would examine this problem here mainly from the point of view of typology.

Although the OCP sites of the Doab show certain common features, the ceramic assemblages suggest their classification into broad groups, A and B. The OCP of Group A is characterised by a composite ceramic tradition suggesting the commingling of the (i) surviving Harappan, (ii) Cemetery-H, and (iii) non-Harappan and non-Cemetery-H elements, as at Ambkheri. Group B is distinguished by predominance of the last category of elements and is almost free from the other two categories of wares, i.e., the Harappan and Cemetrey-H, as at Atranjikhera, Saipai, etc. The Group A includes almost all the shapes enumerated earlier, except nos. 5,14,15,16, and 17 in the above list, while Group B is distinguished by the absence of nos. 9,10,11,12, and 18 occurring in Group A. The prevalence of type nos. 5,14,15,16, and 17, unknown to Group A, is a conspicuous feature of Group B. The incised decoration on the external surface met on the vessels of Group B is absent from Group A. These typological differences in the two groups of the OCP are not blurred by the occurrence of some common shapes for their simple and elementary nature. The use of wheel and the absence of any stratigraphical evidence of its gradual evolution precludes the possibility of an independent local origin of the so-called OCP.

A comparative study of the pottery types of both the groups of the OCP throws significant hints on their genesis. The Group A ware shows close affinities with the Bargaon and Alamgirpur wares in most of the types (figs. 3-4; Deshpande, 1967-2; Sharma, 1959). In fact, the Group A is nothing more than the Bargaon ware minus the classical Harappan shapes, of course, if we overlook the accidental character of the state of preservation in case of the former. All the three ceramic traditions of OCP comprising Group A are present at Bargaon and Alamgirpur. It is for this reason that M.N. Deshpande and Krishna Deva recognise the association of OCP at both the sites in the Harappan complex. Ambkheri represents a decadent stage having limited Harappan traits.

The ceramic industry noticed at Bargaon and Alamgirpur is a widely distributed late Harappan ceramic tradition of north India representing a composite phase of culture pointed out by me elsewhere (Suraj Bhan, 1967). This pottery has been discovered as far west as Katpalon near Jullundur (Dikshit, 1967; 1969) and as far south as Mitathal near Bhiwani excavated by me in 1968 (Suraj Bhan, 1969). In the north, it extends to the Siwalik hills at Bara (Sharma, 1954: 1955) Dher Majra (Olaf Pruefer, 1952; Sharma, 1954), and in the east to Manpur and Bhatpura (R.C. Sharma, 1961; Y.D. Sharma, 1961). A stratigraphical context to this ware has been provided by the excavation at Mitathal and new light thrown on its genesis by it.

In this connection I may mention the ancient site of Siswal (29° 10′N. lat; 75° 30′E. long.) at a distance of 26 km. to the west of Hissar on the left bank of Chautang, identified with the Drishadvati. An exploratory digging at the site by me in 1970, revealed a sequence of two phases called A and B and comparable respectively with pre-Harappan and Harappan periods of Kalibangan. Phase A is characterised by typical Kalibangan fabrics, use of white pigment in addition to black on red surface and the occurrence of incised decoration on the interior of troughs or basins. Phase B, confined to the top levels of the site, is distinguished by a sturdier pottery evolved from early Siswal tradition. It is painted in black monochrome and has a paucity of shapes and painted designs.

The excavations at Mitathal revealed two periods: I and II. Period II was further subdivided into two phases: IIA and IIB. Period I is characterised by late Siswal, i.e., Siswal B, or late Kalibangan ware. Although all the six fabrics of Kalibangan (Lal and Thapar, 1965) are represented in the period, the more common are Fabrics A and C. The pottery is distinguished by a comparatively thick and sturdier variety painted generally with black bands over matt surface in black. The use of white pigment as noticed at Kalibangan or Siswal A ware is conspicuous by its absence. The thick troughs decorated with incised design on the interior are rare. The ceramic types and designs are evolved and lack variety.

Period IIA at Mitathal is characterised by the appearance of Harappan culture. The Harappan pottery contains its classical shapes like dish-on-stand, beaker, perforated jar, tall vase with pointed base, and the vase with beaded rim, raised neck and globular body. Painting is mainly confined to horizontal black bands over light red slip. It is significant that the late Siswal or Siswal B tradition of ceramic industry survives side by side throughout the period unlike at Kalibangan.

Period IIB is marked by a gradual decline in the ceramic traditions of the previous period. The classical Harappan shapes, like the dish-on-stand, beaker, perforated jar and dish with nail-headed rim gradually become less popular. Squattish and sturdy dish-on-stand with hooked rim and drooping rim, vase with beaked or beaded and under-cut rim are the common shapes of Harappan derivation. Besides, the loop handle of vase, vase with flaring rim and vase with flanged rim (Bara type) and bowls with convex sides, tapering sides or carinated profile and featureless, thick, blunted and flattish everted, out-curved rims and basins with flaring, thickened, projected rims contain the Siswal ceramic tradition in this phase. A few shapes simulating the Cemetery-H types, such as dish-on-stand with flaring rim and sharp carinated shoulder and a ridge below the base of dish, jar with collared rim, flask, dish-on-stand with beaded and under-cut rim are also obtained from the site. The incised decoration on the external surface of the pots similar to that at Bara also occurs. The phase is marked by an exuberance of shapes and painted designs suggesting an almost resurgence of Siswal tradition.

The most significant of the associated finds of this phase from the upper levels are the copper implements, such as a flat celt, a ring comparable with those from Bargaon, Bahadrabad and Pondi and *parasu* comparable with one found in the Khurdi hoard from Nagaur district of Rajasthan (Sankalia and others, 1961) and from Daimabad I (Deshpande, 1959). A copper harpoon, almost identical with the one from Saipai, was recovered earlier from the surface at Mitathal near the trench yielding the above tools and its association with them seems quite probable on circumstantial grounds.

Thus, we have seen that *the Bargaon ceramic industry, and for that reason the OCP of Group A, evolved from the fusion of the Harappan and the Kalibangan (pre-Harappan) or Siswal traditions*, a process which had already begun in Mitathal IIA, with a little sprinkling of Cemetery-H traits in the post-Harappan turmoil and eastward movement of people from at least northern Rajasthan forced by the growing dessication of the region due to hydrological changes (Suraj Bhan, 1970). The horizontal expansion of this vertically emerging Harappa-dominated composite culture gradually shed off the classical Harappan elements till they were rendered as destitute as the OCP people of Group A.

The OCP of Group B, on the other hand, shows a fair amount of typological similarity with the late Siswal ware. The OCP types, nos. 1, 2, 3, 4, 5, 6, 7, 8, 13, 14 and 16 (p... above) are either similar to the late Siswal ware at Siswal, Mitathal, Sarangpur and other sites in the Sarasvati basin or are derivable from it. The excavations at Siswal and Mitathal have proved beyond doubt that the Siswal ware evolved through Siswal B or Mitathal I independently and later in a subservient form along with the Harappans. The horizontal extension of Siswal B ware, as known from the explorations carried out by me in the Sarasvati basin, shows that the ware extended from Sarangpur, near Chandigarh (Suraj Bhan, 1967) in the north, to Tigrana near Bhiwani in the south, and from Bani on the right bank of the Ghaggar near Rajasthan border in the west to Rukhi near Gohana and Baliana near Rohtak (information from Shri Silak Ram of Kurukshetra University). The explorations also revealed a concentration of Siswal ware sites in the lower Drishadvati and Yamuna valleys (old bed near Mitathal), and there is less classical Harappan influence in this part. *Thus the probability has been raised for a continuus evolution of the Siswal ware independent of the Harappan influence in the south-eastern parts of Haryana and further east in the lower Doab, which for no better reason than the state of preservation has been called the OCP.* In fact, this term was used by me for the ill-preserved and rolled late Siswal ware of Sarangpur having similar shapes. The examples of ill-preserved and rolled late Siswal ware are not wanting in the Sarasvati basin, which explains the peculiarity of the OCP. The late date for this group of OCP is suggested by the occurrence of evolved types like the vase with a flanged rim (no. 3) and bowl with blunted rim (no. 5) or flaring rim (no. 6) recalling the Mitathal IIB types and the occurrence of an identical harpoon at Mitathal and Saipai.

So far as the nomenclature of the OCP is concerned, it has nothing to commend about it but for its usage. The term signifies only a superfluous and perhaps accidental aspect of the state of preservation of the ceramic industry. It is bound to create more confusion in the already complex cultural mileu of the region by its indiscriminate use by amateurs in the field. Since the cultural complexes of the Groups A and B of the OCP are now best represented at Ambkheri and Atranjikhera respectively, it is suggested to designate the two groups of the OCP after the names of these sites, where their cultural elements are best known.

Y. D. Sharma

I must own that each time I hear or see in print the term Ochre Colour Ware or OCP, I get a little confounded. When B.B. Lal surmised that the ill-fired, thick, ochre-washed pottery at Bisauli and Rajpur Parsu was likely to have been associated with the Copper Hoards found at these two sites, and that the ceramic industries of the lowest levels at Hastinapura might belong to the same class, which was christened by him as Ochre-Coloured Ware (Lal, 1947; 1954-55), he had very good reasons for holding that view in the absence of adequate data, particularly because he had only two clear shapes before him (fig. 5), and neither of these is such that it may be described unique or specialised. Lal certainly did not intend, if I understand him aright, that the term could be used for all red wares, which looked ill-fired, thick and worn-edged. He associated it with the Gangetic Copper Hoards, and thus limited its connotation. But with the Copper Hoards throwing out a challenge, we were floating helplessly midstream and tried to hang on to any straw that came our way. The practice that followed, therefore, was that any ill-defined, soft-fired, worn-edged, porous red ware, found in a likely copper tool association, was described as Ochre Colour Ware or OCP. Even a stalwart like H. D. Sankalia surmised that the red ware associated with copper tools at Nasik, Jorwe, Navasa and Navada Toli was like that of Gangetic sites (Sankalia, 1962, p. 225). I also recollect that unrecognizable Harappan sherds from Ropar (earlier spelt, Rupar, but spelling now revised by Punjab State), when first collected by my colleagues in the Archaeological Survey, were described by them as OCP. The entire range of red ware in the upper Ganga-Yamuna Doab came to be labelled as OCP, if it appeared to precede the Painted Grey Ware. If one could associate copper with it, that set the final seal on the categorization, even where a Harappan context was clear as daylight. In the Doab, upper and central, matters as they stand today, we have five categories of OCP: (i) Harappan, and those found at (ii) Bahadrabad, (iii) Atranjikhera, (iv) Lal-Qila, and (v) Saipai.

In 1961, I had drawn attention to the likeness between Bahadrabad and Harappan wares and felt that the so called ochre-washed or coloured ware was thus only a phase of Harappan ware (Sharma, 1961). It is in that context that I suggested that the pottery from Bahadrabad could perhaps be called Bahadrabad ware. All OCP was not to be named Bahadrabad ware.

Alamgirpur, Bhatpura, Manpur, Ambkheri, Bargaon and a host of other sites in Bulandshahar, Meerut, Muzzaffarnagar and Saharanpur districts have already revealed clear Harappan or related affinities, and no purpose is served by labelling pottery from them as OCP. Bahadrabad's claim for being assigned the same niche is not very clear, and we could perhaps still call it as belonging to the OCP class, as defined by Lal. Atranjikhera has not yielded any specialised Copper Hoard tool, and with its variety of shapes, painted and incised designs (fig. 6), as an assemblage it is outside the Bahadrabad repertoire. Lal-Qila (fig. 7), again as an assemblage, does not tally with Bahadrabad, but some of its painted motifs have correspondence with those of Bara. The pottery from Saipai, selected specimens of which are on exhibit today (fig. 20), qualifies the test of being soft-fired, thick, worn-edged, porous and possessing generally shades of red colour, but is totally different from that of Bahadrabad, although it has some shapes which could be compared with those of Atranjikhera and Lal-Qila. In fact, Saipai, singularly qualifies the test for the title of OCP, having yielded typical Copper Hoard artefacts as well, even if its pottery technically is devoid of ochre colour.

If Harappan sites are eliminated, we are left only with Bahadrabad, Atranjikhera, Lal-Qila and Saipai as contenders for the title of sites yielding OCP. But do we have justification enough for linking them together under the same banner ? This is difficult to answer in 'yes' or 'no'. Yes, if we understand from OCP any worn-edged, soft-fired, porous pottery occurring or believed to occur with Copper Hoards. Atranjikhera and Lal-Qila have not so far yielded Copper Hoard tools, and the pottery from neither of them tallies *as an assemblage* either with Bahadrabad or Saipai. It is under no account a satisfactory solution. *I plead, therefore, that if we are to use the term OCP in definite Copper Hoard context, let us apply the term only for Saipai or sufficiently comparable pottery, and not for others. For others, let us use the term 'ochre colour pottery' or 'ochre colour ware', without the use of capitals, and name the type site Bahadrabad, Atranjikhera, Lal-Qila or Saipai, with which the pottery agrees most, within brackets.* At Saipai, the association of Copper Hoard implements and pottery is certain, but we are not so certain in regard to Bahadrabad, where some of the Copper Hoard implements may have found their way as a trade commodity. The absence of the likely cult object of anthropomorph at Bahadrabad may have significance in this connection.

My views on nomenclature and culture-contact situations of the OCP are covered by what I have said so far. There is not much to add on origin and diffusion. The OCPs of upper and central Doab, if the former may still be called OCP, have not much in common, and so separate zones have to be postulated for both of them. I agree with S. P. Gupta (p. 7, above), however, that Copper Hoards have an east to west movement, although I feel that for the present the specialised Gangetic types cannot be related with those in Bihar or further east. It appears that the upper Doab Harappan and Copper Hoard cultures are contemporary, and as such the lower end of the latter could be postulated to *circa* 2000 B.C. Perhaps 2000-1700 B.C. would be a tentative workable bracket.

Earlier I had mentioned that some colleagues have linked the OCP with Bara. I am taking this opportunity to clarify the position of Bara, as a result of re-assessment. It is given to many to demolish the edifices erected by others. But I am happy that I have to pull down an edifice that I myself raised and begin construction afresh.

This is, however, with very good reason and for better understanding of the sequence of cultures on the Sutlej and the upper Ganga-Yamuna Doab. I had earlier identified three distinct phases of Harappan culture on the upper Sutlej : Kotla Nihang Khan, as the earliest, Ropar coming next and Bara last, although I pointed out that some of the painted designs of pre-Harappan Kalibangan had a 'family likeness' with those of Bara (Sharma, 1964, p. 9; 1965, p. 133). Currently, I am engaged in studying pottery from Bara. *I find that Bara is a single culture site, with Harappan contacts limited to the upper levels. In the lower phase, the pottery is all non-Harappan (figs. 8-10) and pre-Harappan in so far as the tradition in Sutlej valley is concerned.* In the upper phase, the earlier types continue, but there is contact with Harappan traditions. The Harappan pottery is, however, extremely limited (fig. 11), typologically and in quantity, and as such indicates nothing more than a contact. This is substantially different from my earlier interpretation.

I have not yet opened material from Kotla Nihang Khan and Ropar, so that these sites could also be re-assessed. *But I am inclined to think that Harappans were preceded by other folk on the Sarasvati, Drishadvati and the Sutlej. On the Sarasvati mainly were the Kalibangans, on the Drishadvati perhaps the Sothi people, and on the Sutlaj the Bara people.* If the Bara people had some tussle with the Harappans, no definite evidence to that effect is so far available. Apparently, soon both learnt to live together, however. This accounts for occurrence of Bara and Harappan ceramics together from the same levels in the Sutlej valley and the Doab. At Kotla Nihang Khan, 3 km. from Bara, Bara pottery occurs with the Harappan from the lowest levels, but is very small in quantity; at Ropar much more, limited contact with classical pre-Harappan Kalibangan tradition is also discernible in the lower levels of Ropar.

Evidently, this picture is not much different from what we find in West Pakistan, at Amri and Kot Diji, where a pre-Harappan habitation precedes the Harappan.

Bara has common elements not only with pre-Harappan Kalibangan, but also with Amri, Kot Diji and other Baluchistan sites, including particularly Togau and Periano Ghundai. But let me emphasise it, it is the painted motifs and designs that are common and not the shapes. In fact, in painted designs, parallels can be traced further west even to Iran and Iraq.

Apparently, it is the integrated Bara-Harappa folk who moved into the upper Ganga-Yamuna Doab. In fact, they appear to have become one people on the Sutlej itself. I am not aware of even one site on the Sutlej with unmixed classical Harappan ceramics, And, although I have not yet studied the Doab material in detail, it appears to me that there again no site is known exhibiting only Harappan objects without an admixture of Bara elements. As matters stand at present, among sites known to me on the Sutlej and in the upper Doab, Kotla Nihang Khan alone has a high percentage of Harappan pottery.

Whether the common elements between Kalibangan and Bara originate from direct contact or from a common source it is difficult to say at present. The latter possibility has, however, a better case, as the parallels between Bara and Kalibangan are usually limited to painted motifs. Among the six classes of fabrics of Kalibangan (Lal and Thapar, 1965), A, C and E are missing altogether at Bara. The rustication of Fabric B exists, but without painting on it. D alone as a class occurs at Bara, although the type is restricted to troughs and basins. Kalibangan's F is grey or grey-slipped, but Bara's grey ware is neither so fine nor painted, apart from being very limited in quantity.

The integration of Harappans and Bara people appears to have taken place not at or near Ropar, but somewhere downstream and perhaps over a wide region. The sites in Jullundur and Ludhiana districts betray this integration, not excluding Sanghol and Chandigarh, which have been or are being excavated by the Punjab Archaeological Department. Mitathal, district Hissar, excavated by Suraj Bhan (Suraj Bhan, 1969) reveals a similar story, with some variation. It looks also likely that the integration was not only between Harappans and Bara people, but embraced also other contemporary folk, who are yet to be properly identified. In fact, before we succeed in working out the exact nature of this integration, much more field-work is called for.

K. K. Sinha

Presently OCP has been recovered from more than one group of sites. We do not have as yet a corpus of types as known from Atranjikhera, Bahadrabad and

Ambkheri. My own impression is that the Atranjikhera group stands on a different footing in matter of type and fabric than that of Bahadrabad and Ambkheri, where the shapes show a continuity of Harappan tradition.

It is, therefore, apparent that we are dealing with more than one entity of OCP. The usage of a common term OCP for the divergent groups is likely to give the erroneous impression that OCP is a homogeneous type which it obviously is not. I would, therefore, plead for a preparation of corpus of types, and this should be followed by a comparative study. Till then it would be safe to have different names for the different groups. I am inclined to agree with the suggestion of Y.D. Sharma that we should invariably mention the name of the site after the term OCP, e.g., OCP (Atranjikhera) or OCP (Bahadrabad).

R. S. Mittal

I am extremely thankful for the invitation extended to me. I am neither an archaeologist, nor a historian, and therefore, I must express my ignorance of what you have talked about the OCP. With this background, I may inform you that my interest in archaeology arose only in 1962, when the anti-Biotic project at Rishikesh was set up. We in the Department of Geology were asked to investigate the foundations, where the project buildings were to come up. About 300 m. away from the Ganga, at a depth of 3·5 m. we found burnt bricks, measuring 32×38 cm., which were somewhat comparable in colour to red ochre. We requested the Geological Survey of India to pass these bricks on to the appropriate authorities in the Archaeological Survey of India.

The topography of the site is that there is some sort of an island where the river is flowing. If you walk from the water to the plains side, you will find three contours. On the lowest terrace, within 100 m. of water, is situated a temple built with the same kind of bricks which were encountered just below the foot of the hill. Now, I do not know if the bricks are older or the temple.

Geologically speaking, some of my friends think that the desert is moving towards U.P. If you study the deposits, as you travel down from the *Terai* region, you first find rounded stones in the form of boulders. Before you reach coarse sand, you find clay deposits, which may be responsible for some sort of kink in the Ganga in the plains and also in the Yamuna near Delhi. The most important thing is that this area has been affected by floods and quite a number of villages were washed away. The same sort of thing has happened elsewhere. In the year 1880, the river Kali flowed through Nepal by the side of Brahmdeo. It was a very flourishing centre. Today, if you go there, there is nothing of this name. It has obviously been washed away. *So there appears no reason why we should not accept the theory that certain areas were flooded in the past.*

To return to the problem at hand, take a *surahi* or *ghara.* Keep it for the summer and the rainy season. What happens in September or October ? It peels sometime in September. You can yourself judge when the peeling off of pottery occurs. It is due to weathering. *The OCP's appearance could also be due to similar weathering.*

The next point is Rajasthan desert, which falls in the age group between 12,000 and 15,000 years. If the geography of a sub-continent changes, how is it that the history in the different parts of the country, revealing a fundamental geographical change, is placed only within 5,000 years ?

Now I refer again to those bricks. I am told that they belong to the Kushan Period. The temple may have been built with these old bricks, although a Bengali *Sadhu* told me that the temple belonged to the first century B.C. .

M. N. Deshpande (Chairman)

I am glad to find that the discussion has been very fruitful within the limitations of time. I would make a few general comments and then request Shri A. Ghosh to make further observations and wind up the session.

About nomenclature there are two views : one, that the present nomenclature should not be changed and the other that since there are regional differences within the culture, each regional culture may be distinguished and designated separately. I feel that the best way would be to keep the OCP label as it is and add the site name when we are talking of a particular site, for example OCP. (Bahadarabad) or OCP (Atranjikhera).

In my opinion, the OCP (Ambkheri) while sharing the fabric of the corresponding pottery from Atranjikhera and Saipai, differs from it in form but on the other hand the assemblage shows certain affinities with the material of western Uttar Pradesh and eastern Punjab. Among the probable links may be mentioned terracotta cakes, terracotta humped bull and a few pottery shapes like the dish-on-stand, bowl-like-lid with central knob, and cord impressed and incised decorated pottery. The influence of Cemetery-H culture is also seen on the pottery (Deshpande, 1965). Dikshit has traced some connection even with Bara (Dikshit, 1969). About the origin and the mature nature of this culture, its development in time and space, more work is called for. We have to take up the subject seriously. As a first step I would suggest that within the next three months, each one of the excavators, who was responsible for excavation of an OCP site, should give sufficient plates of pottery found by him, with a brief note about the ancillary cultural material, so that we are able to prepare a sort of working paper on the subject, and can further base our conclusion which should be published as a report of the seminar.

To this may be added a few appendices giving bibliography and brief notes on work done by scholars not present here but who have done work on this problem. This will bring out differences in cultural outfit in different regions and it will then be possible to proceed further in determining the question of origin and diffusion.

The other point namely the study of metal technology which Agrawal has put forward is also very important (Agrawal, 1970). The study of the source of copper, if we can trace it—and it may be connected to a certain type of mine—will go a long way. Another thing is that a few more OCP sites should be very systematically excavated under very controlled conditions. Further work at sites like Saipai, and Gadharona is called for. I think some sort of working plan should be prepared, so that universities, the Archaeological Survey of India and State Departments may co-operate and the result should be published as expeditiously as possible.

Certainly more field work and more publication of the material should be accompanied by laboratory work on soil samples. We do not know whether it was one flood, or many floods, or long exposure and transportation of sediments by winds that was responsible for the nature of the cultural deposit one come across in the excavation. All these can be worked out after a series of soil analysis. After all, in this discussions, I feel, we are not groping in the dark. Systematic work is bound to place this culture in proper time-sequence and help us in understanding the panorama of cultures of the Gangetic valley. In any case, the discussion has been very fruitful and I thank every one of the participants for his valuable contribution.

A. Ghosh (General President)

It is time for us to take up the next item of the agenda. I would like to make a few observations, though I must admit that very little remains to be said after the most interesting discussion we have had.

We began with an undertone. There was one OCP culture initially. The Chairman then said that there was a Gangetic culture and a Yamuna culture: and Dikshit and Suraj Bhan spoke of groups A and B. Nigam has put in four groups;

Sharma as many as five groups in the Doab. Apart from the superficial texture of the pottery, there appears nothing that has been said about the identity of the culture. We are not sure whether it represented one culture or many phases of one culture or there were several entirely different cultures altogether. Now before we establish an identity, to name a culture is certainly very premature. If we go on ascribing the OCP to Europeans or Assyrians this does not solve the problem. Similarly the name also is admittedly unsatisfactory, in the absence of link. Still, unless some definite and satisfactory solution is found, it is difficult to my mind to change the name. But I would certainly agree with Dr. Sharma that we give up using capital letters for Ochre Colour Ware or Pottery, so that nobody is allowed to believe that we are referring to coloured pottery like red ware without emphasis or any implications, though it is having implications. Addition of the name of the site where it is found may be helpful.

SESSION ON NBP

K. K. Sinha (Chairman)

I am very thankful to the authorities of the Indian Archaeological Society for asking me to take the chair over the session of this seminar on the nomenclature of NBP Ware and other allied issues. As you all know, the need for the present symposium arose as a result of deliberations held at Nagpur during the course of the meeting of the Indian Archaeological Society in 1970. It has been generally felt that the name Northern Black Polished Ware is no longer valid in the present context and that the time has come for changing it. It was against this background that the Nagpur meeting decided to refer the matter for a detailed consideration at a future date. It is now our duty to subject the issue to as thorough an examination as possible.

The NBP is in a better position than the OCP. It is much more widely known, and it is not restricted to a comparatively small region, as is the case with the OCP. We are fortunate in having Shri A. Ghosh here with us to guide the proceedings. He was associated with the excavations at Ahichchhatra in the early forties, and the article on the pottery from Ahichchhatra published by him jointly with K. C. Panigrahi, featured for the first time the occurrence of the NBP Ware (Ghosh and Panigrahi, 1946).

As the one charged with the burden of initiating the discussion, I deem it my duty to present before you both sides of the picture, i.e., arguments favouring a change as well as those which favour a *status quo*. It will be up to the members present here to decide one way or the other. Arguments favouring a change are fairly well known. One of the familar jibes is that it is neither 'northern', nor 'black', nor 'polished'. The ware is no longer confined to the Gangetic plains and has been reported from several sites in central and western India and is known to have occurred at Amaravati in Andhra Pradesh In the face of this evidence the term 'northern' loses its validity. Similarly, it is said that the term 'black' does not do full justice to a ware which occurs in shades other than black. As for the term 'polished', it is generally agreed that the lustrous surface of the ware was not achieved by polishing, and hence the term 'polished' is a misnomer. In short, we have gone a long way since mid-forties when the ware was given its present name. On the present reckoning, therefore, the ware needs to be given a name which may more appropriately reflect its changed status acquired as a result of field-investigations over the past two decades.

When we proceed to change a term like the NBP, which has been in use over a long period, one of the questions that we have to face is how easy it will be for a new term to gain currency. If we are to be faced with a situation in which both the old and new terms are being used concurrently, you will agree that this will lead to an avoidable confusion. In this context, I have been urged by some of my friends the instance of the decision some years back to change the terms Series I, Series II and Series III to Early Stone Age, Middle Stone Age and Late Stone Age. I concede that no such difficulty has been experienced in the implemention of the changed nomenclature of the Stone Age industries. At the same time, we have to realise that the study of the Stone Age industries is confined to a fairly restricted number of scholars and the acceptance and usage of a modification in terminology does not present any difficulty. As against this, the NBP Ware, a cardinal artefact of the early historical period, has been with us for well over two decades and a changed label is not likely to find a universal acceptance. But this certainly cannot be turned into an excuse for retaining the term If we decide to change the term, each one of us here present, I am sure, will do his best to get as wide a currency for the new term as lies within one's means. It is at this very moment that I urge you to look at the other side of the picture and let us ask ourselves : 'is the case for retaining the present name defenceless ?' It is in the context of this question that I am making a few observations.

We shall first take up the question of geographical limit imposed by the term 'northern'. It is true that the ware has been reported from several sites in central and western India and from the Deccan. At the same time we cannot lose sight of the fact that outside the Gangetic plains, there is not a single site which has yielded the NBP Ware in any considerable numbers. Except perhaps Ujjain, where the ware has distinctly an inferior quality as compared to its counterparts in the north, the ware is reported to be restricted in numbers everywhere in central and western India. Those of us who have had the experience of working on sites like Sravasti, Kausambi, Vaisali, Rajgir and Rajghat are struck by the dominating position of the NBP in the contemporary levels both in regard to numbers and shapes. This position is in marked contrast to the one noticed on sites south of Vindhyan plains, where its occurrence in insignificant numbers had led scholars to suspect that the ware might be an import from the Gangetic north. That the ware originated in the middle Ganga plains has never been in doubt. If, therefore, we take into account the origin and major centres of dispersal of the ware as our guidelines, is there any harm in retaining the term 'northern' ? This is the question that we have to decide.

As stated earlier, doubts have been raised about retaining the term 'black' as the ware has been known to have occurred in a variety of shades other than black. Here I may be permitted to draw upon my experience of working on the collection of NBP from my dig at Sravasti. I am in a postion to state that more than 80 percent of the specimens were quite definitely black. This, I believe, will be true of other sites as well. On this reckoning alone, there does not appear to be any justification for doing away with the term 'black'.

At this point, I should also like to draw your attention to the fact that many specimens of the variations in colour may not be intentional. There are three categories of colour variations :

i. Intentional black or other colour,
ii. Accidental non-black, and
iii. Intentional non-black.

I have no hesitation in stating that quite a substantial percentage, perhaps more than 80 percent of the total collection of the NBP, comes under the first category. This would leave only an insignificant minority of specimens which might have been intended to be non-black. Colour variations ranging over deep black, steel grey, blueish black and blue burnished black, can result from kiln conditions. I have, thus, no doubt in my mind that in dealing with the NBP, we are dealing with an essentially black ware, whether we call it Northern Black Ware or Indian Black Ware. The term 'black' need not be changed.

Finally, we come to the term 'polished'. The term is misleading inasmuch as we know that the surface lusture of the NBP was not achieved as a result of polishing. Although many investigations have been carried out, so as to determine the nature of the surface lusture, no satisfactory explanation has as yet been possible. While I do not particularly favour retaining the term 'polished', I do wish to make a plea for having some term which could distinguish the NBP Ware specimens from many others which are very near to NBP in every other respect except for the shining lusture. Howsoever imperfect the term 'polished' may be, it does give an indication of the resultant effect as distinguished from the 'cause'. In the absence of a substitute which has to await a final verdict from the chemist on the nature of the surface lusture, the word 'polished' may continue to serve the limited purpose, though very imperfectly indeed.

It is for you all to decide whether we wish to change the name or maintain the *status quo.* If we decide to do away with the existing name, our next task will then be to find a substitute name.

Evidence from Sravasti and Ahichchhatra, and in an indirect way from Atranjikhera and Alamgirpur, confirms that there was a stage of overlap between the Painted Grey and NBP Wares. I think it will be a good thing if this gathering were to affirm this position categorically, since the impression still persists that the NBP succeeds the PGW without an overlap anywhere in the stratigraphic sequence of the Gangetic north. In this connection, I wish to draw your pointed attenion to a paper by me entitled 'The NBP Ware—Fresh hypothesis in the light of Sravasti evidence—' presented at the seminar on potteries in ancient India held under the auspices of the Patna University (Sinha, 1969).

I may repeat for the benefit of you all very briefly some of the salient points in regard to the stratigraphy and chronology. The NBP Ware cannot by itself be regarded as a safe datable criterion, as it is known to have occurred in widely differing contexts. This is important, since still excavators continue to depend on the mere occurrence of NBP specimens for the dating of levels. Among the sites where NBP has a definitely earlier datable contexts are Rajgir, Vaisali, Rajghat, Sravasti, Kausambi and Taxila. Here it belongs mainly to a date bracket of 550-250 B.C. Sites like Hastinapur, Charsada, Kumrahar and perhaps Ropar and Ujjain belong to a later date bracket (350-150 B.C).

The question of diffusion is not easy to answer particularly at this stage of our knowledge, when not much is know about pre-NBP deposits in eastern U.P. and Bihar. A few relevant observations may be made in this connection. On the basis of the present evidence, the main productive region of the NBP is formed by a rough rectangle whose western arm is formed by a line joining Vaisali and Rajgir. It was in this region that the NBP Ware originated and we also notice the occurrence in lowest levels of the most representative specimens retaining in full measure the brilliant lustrous surface. The question as to how did it all happen is not easy to answer. If the pre-NBP deposits in the region do not hold the answer, the possibility of a diffusion cannot be ruled out.

While considering the question of diffusion, I wish to draw your attention to points of similarity between PGW and NBP Wares. The highly striking surface lusture of the NBP tends to obliterate the points of apparent similarity between the two wares. There is a near identity of shapes between the two wares; the core is grey in both the cases and thinness of the body is a feature common to both. The difference between the two appears to be confined only to the surface treatment—the painting of the PGW giving way to the lusture of the NBP Ware. As the PGW had an earlier history in the region;, the possibility of a wholesale diffusion is at once ruled out. A partial diffusion of technique resulting in the surface lusture of NBP is all that we can think of. I am not in a position to elaborate it any further in view of the paucity of evidence.

Y. D. Sharma

Although the NBP is not an accurate description for the ware denoted by it, its continued use creates no confusion in identifying the particular ware, and as such I do not see any necessity for changing the nomenclature now.

That there is an overlap between the PGW and NBP is also borne out by my small-scale excavation at Khalaua, district Agra, where a single NBP sherd occurred in an upper horizon of predominantly PGW levels.

Dr. Sinha's placement of Ropar in the later date bracket (i.e., 350-150 B.C.) runs counter to a C^{14} date obtained from lower levels of the NBP period. On the basis of 5730 ± 40 as half-life of radiocarbon and assuming 1950 as the 'present' year, it works out to 485 ± 100 B.C. Thus even if we agree with Dr. Sinha in assuming two contexts for the NBP, the Ropar NBP would appear to go with his earlier context.

N. C. Ghosh

There is a phase of NBP which is free from the PGW as clear from excavations at Purana-Qila and Hastinapura. In the western part of northern India, PGW dominated, whereas in the eastern part the NBP occupied a similar position.

The origin of the NBP should be searched somewhere in mid-eastern India, around Pataliputra. At Chirand, in the upper phase of the chalcolithic culture, i.e., in Period II, there is a highly polished black ware reminiscent of the NBP, and this could be the precursor of the NBP.

From east the NBP travelled west, whereas the PGW penetrated from west to east. This resulted in an overlap of the two wares at certain sites.

R. C. Gaur

Though the C^{14} dates now available to us for the NBP range between second to fifth centuries B.C., an earlier antiquity of the industry is also possible on the basis of stratigraphic study of the NBP deposits at Kausambi (Sharma, 1960), Sravasti (Sinha, 1967) and Atranjikhera (Gaur, 1968; 1969). It may be possible that while the pottery flourished as a developed industry from fifth century B. C. onward, its manufaturing started on experimental basis long ago, probably a century or even more earlier. This assumption needs a careful study, particularly at such sites which have the NBP and the pre-NBP deposits without any break. It may also be possible that the industry might have been introduced by the potters at a site in the PGW area, where iron was already in use, and later on after its 'know-how' spread, it flourished at its known epicentres located in the region of the iron-fields. However, this suggestion is absolutely hypothetical, since the emergence of the NBP from the black-slipped ware, an earlier pottery of the NBP region, is also plausible.

On Sravasti and Atranjikhera evidence the NBP period may broadly be divided into two phases: (i) pre-Mauryan, and (ii) Mauryan. The excavator of Sravasti has classified them as (i) pre-structural, and (ii) structural.

However, at Atranjikhera on material evidences it may be termed as belonging to (i) pre-defence, and (ii) defence deposits. This nomenclature became necessary for Atranjikhera deposits, since a large number of iron objects occurred in the earlier phase which evidenced structural activity. Moreover, properly laid-out bricks were also encountered in this phase occasionally, although on the whole the structural activity in this phase was of an insignificant nature.

D. P. Agrawal

Literally speaking, the NBP is a misnomer. But by association it has assumed the sanctity of a name for the ware we know as the NBP. Changing a name at this stage would, therefore, add to confusion. We should instead address ourselves to more important problems concerning the NBP.

The C^{14} dates have clearly shown that the PGW has a time-spread of 800-400 B.C., whereas the NBP shows 550-50 B.C. bracket. It is obvious, therefore, that ereht was an overlap between the two wares from fourth to sixth centuries B.C. It is further borne out by the common red ware shapes that are associated with the NBP in the eastern sites and with the PGW in the western Doab. It would make a very interesting study to go into the changes of the associated wares and other repertoire of the NBP as it spread westward, and of the PGW as it advanced eastward.

The apparent affinity of the NBP and the PGW is due to the use of the same fine alluvial clay of the Gangetic valley. Otherwise, the PGW is western in origin and is a painted pottery tradition with controlled firing to achieve a grey colour of the ware. The NBP, on the other hand, is largely unpainted and has a very distinctive gloss. In their origins both the wares should have distinct identities. Only in the overlap phase could they have influenced each other.

The NBP is distinctively a pre-Mauryan ware. There is a concensus that its origin is eastern. Its epicenter was perhaps Bihar, and it may mark the spread of abundant Bihar iron and consequent colonisation of the wooded Doab in the fifth-sixth centuries B.C.

The distinctive gloss of the NBP has yet to be clearly understood. Hegde thinks that it is due to the use of *Sajji* soil (Hegde, 1966), whereas Dr. B. B. Lal holds that the gloss was produced by putting the hot pot into an organic solution (Lal, 1955-56). The British Museum has given a different view (1959). A concerted work in this direction and convincing reproduction of the gloss in the laboratory will alone solve the mystery of the NBP.

S. P. Gupta

In the Nagpur conference of the Society, Professor Haertel voiced his concern over the continued usage of the term NBP for a ware which, as we now know, was confined neither to northern India, nor to black colour; in fact, it was not polished either. On being asked as to what new term he would like to give to the ware which we have been calling for decades as the NBP, he left the matter to be decided by Indian field-workers.

We all know that an anomaly between the term and the actual character of the ware has existed for long; but we have never been able to replace the term by a new one. To me it appears that there has been a fundamental fallacy in our approach. We have been taking the NBP Ware as a single homogeneous ware produced out of a single technique and comprising a single set of pottery types. I am afraid, this may not be the case. The excavations at Sravasti, Kausambi, etc., have clearly brought to light a number of wares which are associated with the NBP. Although some of these wares are of different shades of red colour, they are as shining as the black wares. Some of these wares bear paintings of different designs produced by different techniques. Obviously, we cannot remove these wares from the fold of the NBP Ware. It appears that the term NBP has outgrown its limits. It is now a big umbrella under which not one but several wares are protected. How can, therefore, any one suggest a single term that may justify the existence of all these wares ?

I, therefore, feel that we do not have many choices; either we retain the term on pragmatic grounds, or we evolve several terms, one for one ware. Since evolving several terms for the NBP Ware complex is too hazardous to be undertaken, I plead for the retention of the term.

M. C. Joshi

The problem of the NBP is not to be studied in isolation as has often been done. The origin and spread of this *de luxe* pottery should be examined in relation to the contemporary metal wares and the trading conditions between the 6th and 2nd centuries B.C. It may be examined whether the disappearance of the NBP was on account of the production of better and cheaper metal utensils. Further, the zonal distribution of the NBP and its associated pottery should also be cerefully studied, in order to check as to in how many cases it was continued to be manufactured in the post-Mauryan times.

It is also desirable to take into account the contemporary literary data in this regard, especially the reference to pottery-making, metallic sound of the earthenware (*Vinaya Pitaka)*, use of slip, burnishing (*Upadi Sutta)*, etc. In this context I would like to refer to Halahala, a woman potter of Sravasti around the 5th century B.C., who is described as a patron of the Ajivaka sect in Pali literature. Does this reference not indicate the prosperity of a potter's family (which was rich enough to patronize a growing non-Brahmanical sect), in the early phase of the urbanization in the Madhya-desa and adjoining areas ? Could we not infer therefrom that the material prosperity of a potter might have depended around the 5th century B.C. on the production of *de luxe* wares like the NBP and its growing demand in the market ?

M. N. Deshpande

The PGW and NBP co-exist for a long time at a number of sites but we must find out when exactly the NBP comes into the picture and when the PGW stops occurring. This is a very crucial point. We do not find prolific use of iron tools in the early levels of PGW. However, NBP ushers a full-fledged use of iron coinciding with the grand emergence of early historical townships with various structures of burnt-bricks and cut timber. The needs of the rich and sophisticated section of the society gave birth to this *de luxe* pottery which may have also been used by religious teachers. Buddhist monks could have perhaps used this pottery; especially the bowl, as could be surmised from the find of this pottery at Buddhist establishments, the southernmost being Amaravati in district Guntur.

As regards surface treatment, it is not only black-polished, but there are also various other shades with the gloss giving golden or silver shine and a few vessels painted with lines on a shining surface. It would be of interest to study if the wares made in this manner served any particular need, e.g., to store acidic substances or other materials.

I feel that the old nomenclature certainly should continue, for the few sherds we get outside northern India were evidently transported there from northern India.

K. N. Dikshit

The NBP ware which was first discovered at Taxila, is essentially the pottery of northern India, although it has been found as far south as Amaravati and Karad. However, a change in nomenclature will create confusion.

The Tata Institute of Fundamental Research, Bombay, has published a number of C^{14} dates of NBP levels, but nowhere the early date has gone beyond 530 B.C. At places, the PGW has been found in the NBP horizon (e.g., Ahichchhatra, Allahapur, Atranjikhera, Ropar, Bairat, etc.). The upper levels are dated to 50 B.C., and even A.D. 130. As most of the early C^{14} dates are round about 400 B.C., I shall like to assign the NBP time bracket between 400 and 50 B.C.

Dr. K. K. Sinha is of the opinion that there are certain primary centres of NBP distribution. He keeps Taxila, a trading centre, in the list of primary centres. I do not know how Dr. Sinha has kept Taxila in the list of primary centres and weeded out other sites of the region also falling on the trade-route connecting Magadha with Balkh (*Uttara-path*). The NBP settlements at Ropar, Indraprastha, Hastinapura and Ahichchhatra cannot easily be separated from Taxila. The presence of Asokan inscriptions in Delhi and in its neighbourhood are clear indication that this area was in close contact with the imperial power at Magadha. In my opinion the whole of north-western India (now Pakistan), including eastern Panjab and western U.P., should come under the list of secondary centres as the NBP seems to have spread in this region with the expansion of the Mauryan empire.

K. K. Sinha (Chairman)

I have now to wind up the discussion. That there was an overlap between the PGW and the NBP is accepted, but the duration of the overlap is not clear. The general feeling is for retaining the present nomenclature.

I have taken two clear stages within which the NBP occurs. The monumental architecture, to which M. N. Deshpande has made a reference, belongs to the later stage. Even at Kausambi and Rajghat well-built structures do not occur before 300 B.C.

To my mind, the PGW and the NBP are very close to each other. With the PGW occurs a black-slipped ware, which is technologically not far from the NBP. Even in point of shapes and varieties, the PGW and the NBP look to be related. I think we can go a long way if both PGW and NBP are subjected to chemical examination and their relationship, if any, worked out.

A. Ghosh (General President)

We had a most interesting and controversial discussion in the afternoon as in the morning. There is a consensus of opinion that no change in the nomenclature of the NBP is called for. The overlap between the PGW and NBP has been established by several excavations, and there are no two opinions about it. Dr. Sinha has stated that there was no break between the two cultures represented by the PGW and the NBP, and I think that this is very logical. About the diffusion of the NBP, to my mind, it is quite clear. At Taxila, as far as I recollect, only 27 sherds of the NBP were found; at Kausambi, in the NBP levels, 50 percent of the sherds belonged to the NBP class. Therefore, its diffusion from eastern U.P. or Bihar is very clear. It has been very rightly pointed out that some advance work has been done regarding its manufacturing technique, but no concentrated research work. This must be attended to. What I feel is that whatever its technique may have been, it must have been very sound. Otherwise, it would be difficult to explain its uniform quality over a large area.

We have covered quite a lot of ground both in the morning and in the afternoon. We may now look forward to see our deliberations in print. Before we disperse, I must thank the Indian Archaeological Society very much for asking me to be present here and preside over today's deliberations.

APPENDIX A

SALVAGE OF ARCHAEOLOGICAL EVIDENCE FROM BAHADRABAD

Y. D. Sharma

In 1951-52, at Bahadrabad, 12 km. west of the headworks of the Ganga Canal at Hardwar, a diversion channel had to be dug up for siting an hydro-electric power-house. The excavators reported the occurrence of some red pottery from considerable depth. On request, they forwarded a few fragmentary sherds to the Archaeological Survey of India, New Delhi. But these could not be identified at the time. Some time later, I thought of examining the site personally, and when I reached there, I was shown a small hoard of copper objects said to have come from the same level as the pottery earlier reported (Krishnaswami, 1953; Sharma, 1961, 1964). I was also able to collect some more pottery from the earth thrown up by the excavators. The Copper Hoard and the red ware made clear sense, as the latter appeared to fall in the same category as the ochre-coloured ware reported earlier by B. B. Lal from Bisauli, Rajpur Parsu and Hastinapura (Lal, 1951; 1954-55). I decided, therefore, to cut down the banks of the diversion channel and salvage such evidence of the cultural strata as was still *in situ*.

Several trenches were laid out at right angles to the channel-bed on both sides of it. After cutting through a thickness of 5.70 m. of alternating sterile layers of sand and pebbles, I struck the familiar red ware. On an average, the occupation layer, consisting of water-soaked compact dark brown clay, measured 0.60 m. in thickness. No copper object came to my hand during these operations, but immediately above the natural soil on the southern flank of the channel lay some quarzite flake tools and waste flakes (Krishnaswami, 1953). Their number is extremely small, and the fact that they occurred only along the lower fringe of the pottery-bearing levels, indicated that they must have been lying there before the arrival of the pottery-using people. V. D. Krishnaswami opines that this industry "belongs to a flake tool complex assignable to two broad facies : (i) cleaver-chopper made on a mammoth lunate reminiscent of a microlithic lunate; and (ii) a jagged wavy-edged scraper formed by a different technique as revealed in the Early to Late Sohan industry".

The pottery is generally thick, soft and, although made from medium-grained well-levigated clay, it shows the addition of fine or coarse sand as *degraissant*. Its colour varies between bright red to terracotta buff, although some pots are fired to a grey colour. Originally it was covered with a thick slip, which stuck to the lumps of clay or peeled off as soon as sherds were extricated from them. With a worn-off surface, the sherds have a rolled appearance. Perhaps 'ill-fired' or 'inadequately fired', as described by me earlier, is not a correct description of the pottery, as it is generally well-burnt. No painting was noticed, and if there were any, they must have gone with the slip. A few sherds had, however, wavy incised decoration, or notchings on cord pattern along the belly. A looped handle was also noticed.

Among the principal pots (figs. 13-14), classified according to use and shape, are jars (nos. 8, 17, 17a, 17b, 17c, 19, 20), vases (nos. 5, 22, 23, 23a 24, 25, 26), bowls (nos. 18, 18a, 19a, 21, 21a, 21b, 27, 28, 29, 30, 31, 32, 33), basins (nos. 4, 4a, 4b, 4c, 4d, 14, 14a) dishes-on-stand (nos. 1, 1a, 7), pedestalled bowls (nos. 3, 3a), a small ring-stand (no. 2), lids with a central knob, (nos. 6, 6a) and small cups or saucers (9, 10, 11, 12, 13).

The problem is, culturally, where does this pottery fit in ? Its association with Copper Hoard objects, although based on surmise and not physically observed by a trained archaeologist, makes us turn naturally to known Copper Hoard sites. Specialised Copper Hoard implements, including harpoons, had been reported from Bisauli and Rajpur Parsu, but pottery excavated there was too fragmentary to produce any definite shapes. From Hastinapura, no copper tool from the OCP level is reported and the pottery shapes recorded from there (fig. 5; Lal, 1954-55), are absent at Bahadrabad. With OCP shapes from Atranjikhera (fig. 6; Gaur, 1967, 1969-2), correspondence, even though not complete, is limited as shown below :-

	Shape	Bahadrabad	Atranjikhera
1.	Narrow-necked jar with flaring rim	Fig. 14, nos. 17, 17b	Fig. 6, nos. 1-2; Gaur, 1969.
2.	Deep bowl with slightly out-covered rim	Fig. 14, no. 33	Fig. 6, nos. 9, 10; Gaur, 1969.
3.	Small lid or bowl with flaring sides and thinning rim.	Fig. 14, no. 32	Fig. 6, no. 11; Gaur, 1969.
4.	Loop handle	Fig. 13, no. 16	Fig. 6, no. 18; Gaur 1969.

There is also at Atranjikhera base of a stem taken to be that of a dish-on-stand, but its features are different from those of Bahadrabad. The notched and incised designs from Atranjikhera do not belong to the same pattern and technique as those from Bahadrabad. Besides, it has also yielded painted pottery, which has not been noticed at Bahadrabad. Largely, therefore, Bahadrabad, and Atranjikhera follow different ceramic traditions.

With Lal-Qila (fig. 7) Bahadrabad has practically nothing to compare among specialised features. The same applies to Baharia, district Shahjahanpur (pp. 42-3; fig. 16) and to Noh, district Bharatpur (pp. 43-4; fig. 17).

Saipai, (Thapar, 1970; Lal, pp. 47-49 figs. 19-20), which has the unique distinction of having yielded a hooked spearhead, harpoon and plain and painted pottery in a systematic excavation, again does not offer any parallels with Bahadrabad in specialised pottery shapes. The only shapes from Bahadrabad which are broadly comparable are narrow-necked jar, with out-curved flaring rim (fig. 14, nos. 17, 17b), vase with beaked rim (fig. 14, no. 24), bowl with thickened but inwardly inclined rim (fig. 14, no. 21) and bowl with out-curved rim (fig. 14, no. 33). A fragment taken to represent the stem of a dish-on-stand is rather dubious.

The net result of the above examination is that Bahadrabad pottery as an assemblage does not tally with known Copper Hoard or OCP sites. It has, however, some parallels in shapes with Bara and certain Harappan sites (fig. 15). Among such shapes are dish-on-stand, pedestalled bowl, lid with central knob, basin with heavily beaded and undercut rim, open based and internally incised basin, small ring-stand, bowl or dish with splayed out rim, globular jar with narrow neck and splayed out rim and vase with long and flaring neck and thickened rim. A jar with a flange below the rim also occurs, but the flange, has a smaller diameter than the mouth and may, therefore, be purely ornamental and not intended to receive a lid as in the Harappan vessel.

The correspondence of Bahadrabad pottery with that of Harappan sites, particularly in the upper Doab led me earlier (Sharma, 1961) to the opinion that the so called ochre-washed or -coloured ware was only a phase of Harappan ware. Later (Sharma, 1965), I felt that the Harappan affinity of Bahadrabad was not so firm. A look at the comparative chart (fig. 15) will show that Bahadrabad's correspondence with Bara is closer than that with Harappan sites.

In this connection, I am tempted to point out that although pottery from Lal-Qila as an assemblage, is different from Harappa or Bara-Harappa complex, certain features do show parallels with Bara pottery. Among these are a vase with a concave neck, lid with splayed out rim and dish with drooping rim. Also comparable are painted motifs like cross-hatched triangles, needled long arch and juxtaposed curved motifs. Among incised designs a parallel is offered by a freeze of hooked sigmas. It is possible, therefore, that more than one tradition go in the make-up of Lal-Qila, and some of these may be that of Bara. Located as it is within the upper Ganga-Yamuna

Doab, it falls within the zone where Bara-Harappa ceramic traditions are clearly discernible.

Where does all this analysis lead us to ? Bahadrabad pottery, considered as a whole, does not fall in the Bara-Harappa complex of the upper Doab represented by Alamgirpur, Ambkheri or Baragaon. It does not tally with Lal-Qila, which exhibits a partial correspondence with Bara. Also with central Doab sites like Atranjikhera and Saipai it shows no direct connection. It appears to possess, however, some relationship with Bara-Harappa complex, even though it is limited and rather remote.

How it it then that a Copper Hoard is found associated with this pottery ? It is quite possible that the Gangetic Copper Hoards were a common property of several people whose ceramic traditions were different from each other. It is also possible and perhaps rather likely, as hinted by me earlier (Sharma, 1965) that we have not yet identified the manufacturers of Copper Hoards. They may be wandering craftsmen like the present-day *gadul lohars* moving their camps in carts from place to place over long distances, and these craftsmen may have supplied the implements to contemporary folks with different ceramic traditions, but common means of livelihood and comparable economic stage of development.

This will also make it easier to explain the occurrence of a fragmentary anthropomorph at distant Lothal (Lohuizen, 1960). For the present apparently we do not have adequate evidence to think of a common Copper Hoard people or culture *on the basis of pottery*, and we must encourage the spade to throw up more clods of earth before the story can be cast in a reasonable frame.

APPENDIX B

EXCAVATIONS AT BAHARIA, DISTRICT SHAHJAHANPUR

G. R. Sharma

The chance discovery of two Copper Hoard implements (pl. I) had been reported from Baharia, about 51.5 km. south-west of the district headquarters of Shahjahanpur. In order to ascertain the nature of the deposit and to establish the relationship, if any, between the Copper Hoard and ochre-coloured pottery found on the surface, a small trial trench, 1. 21 m. sq. was laid out near the find-spot of the Copper Hoard. The excavation was conducted by the Allahabad University. The natural soil was struck at a depth of 1 m. The total habitational deposit was constituted by three layers: Layer (1), 25.4 cm. thick, was composed of hard brownish clay. Layer (2), with a thickness of 45.72 cm., was pale brownish and sandy, while layer (3) with a thickness of 30.48 cm. was dark brownish, imperceptibly merging with the natural soil underneath. On enquiry it was learnt that the copper implements were found at a depth of 91.4 cm. 'below surface, probably the actual spot falling in layer (3).

A few pot-sherds, mostly pale red, having a tendency of rubbing off easily, were found sporadically distributed in all the three layers. In some cases the sherds bear a white encrustation, as a result of which the nature of the slip employed thereon has become obscure. However, in some cases the traces of a dark ochrous slip are visible. Among the types (fig. 16) particular mention may be made of (.) vase with beaded outer rim and concave neck, (2) vase, presumably globular, with flared rim, having a shallow depression on the interior and short constricted neck, (3) vase with splayed out featureless rim, and (4) vase with out-turned externally beaded rim.

The two copper implements, a harpoon and a new type of sword, were obtained from this site while digging clay for preparing bricks. The harpoon, measuring 27·5 cm. in present form, is well preserved and a fine specimen of the type. It has a prominent medial rib and tapering blade, only broken at the tip-end. The middle portion has two pairs of incurved barbs of cylindrical section. The junction of the barbed portion and the tang has been marked by the presence of two knobs, the right one being perforated, evidently for passing a cord. The implement has been made by casting. The sword measuring 45.48 cm. in length, represents in itself an altogether new type in the assemblage of copper implements discovered so far. Like the harpoon described above, it has also got a prominent medial rib and tapering blade. The junction of the blade and hilt is characterised by the presence of a pair of barbs of flat section. From the end of the hilt emanates a hook, evidently made for strengthening the grip. The specimen is undoubtedly the result of casting, though hammering seems to have been done on the hilt and the hook subsequently for finishing them.

APPENDIX C

THE DISCOVERY OF OCHRE COLOURED POTTERY FROM NOH, DISTRICT BHARATPUR

Vijaya Kumar

So far OCP was reported from Hastinapura, Bahadrabad, Ambkheri, Bargaon, Atranjikhera and Ahichchhatra. In Rajasthan, it fell to the lot of Shri R. C. Agrawala,

Director, Archaeology and Museums, to discover it in 1963-64 at Noh, in district Bharatpur (Agrawala, 1967), which is the western limit of the distribution of this pottery (fig. 1). In 1964-65, the present writer took up an area of 12 m. by 15 m. in the OCP levels and noticed that it occupied a separate horizon just above the natural soil and below the black and red ware levels (Vijaya Kumar, 1969). From 1966-67 to 1970-71 each year an area of 5 m. sq. was dug in these levels. The excavations confirmed that OCP constituted Period I of the site.

The date of this pottery has been roughly estimated as 1300 B.C. This estimate is based on two C^{14} dates from the mid-levels of the PGW period (Period III), falling in the 9th and 7th centuries B.C.

The OCP sherds occupy a 0.90 m. thick deposit of brownish clay. Apart from fragments of handles, vases, a basin and a bowl (fig. 17), no complete shapes are available. The sherds are orange to deep red in colour. They are wheel-turned, porous, fragile and treated with a wash. Most of the sherds are thick and the edges rolled.

The range of decoration comprises two varieties, namely, (i) incised, and (ii) applique. Applique type, has a solitary example (no. 4). The incised decoration (no. 2) is similar to that of Atranjikhera. No other finds have been obtained from this deposit till this date.

APPENDIX D

SISWAL: A PRE-HARAPPAN SITE IN DRISHADVATI VALLEY

Suraj Bhan

The excavation at Amri by N. G. Majumdar in 1929 (Majumdar, 1934) for the first time provided stratigraphical evidence of a culture ante-dating the Indus or Harappa civilization. A similar pre-Harappen substratum was discovered at Harappa in 1946 (Wheeler, 1947) and at Kot-Diji in 1955 (Khan, 1958, 1965). The excavations at Kalibangan in the sixties (Lal and Thapar, 1967) have further extended the geographical and cultural horizon of the pre-Harappan culture complex making it more and more necessary to investigate the nature and extent of the pre-Harappan cultural mileu in northern India.

In 1968 the excavations at Mitathal provided stratigraphical evidence for the evolution of pre-historic cultures of the Sarasvati basin from pre-Harappan to late Harappan times (Suraj Bhan, 1969). Mitathal I provided typological ceramic similarities with Kalibangan I, but the two also differed. In the former the ware is rather sturdy, shapes and painted designs scarce and the use of white pigment absent on painted designs. Also there are no microliths. Further, the occurrence of a few Harappan types, like beaker, dish and terracotta cakes suggested a contact of this phase with the Harappans, necessitating thus the investigations if there existed a true pre-Harappan horizon comparable with Kalibangan I in this part of the country. Siswal, where both Kalibangan I and Mitathal I wares were found on the surface, suggested a possibility of throwing light on this aspect. As a consequence, a small exploratory trench was sunk at Siswal during the autumn of 1970.

The village of Siswal (lat. 29.10′N; long. 75.30′E) is located at a distance of 26 km. west of Hissar, district headquarters in Haryana State. It is approached by road from Adampur Mandi, a railway station on the Rewari-Fazilka section of the Northern Railway, about 3 km. to the north.

The site lies about 300 m. to the north of the village along the left bank of the now deserted Hissar Major or the Chautang canal. It is a low mound, 12.5 m. high, covering approximately an area of 300 by 200 m. The site is under cultivation and its north-eastern portion has been much disturbed having been converted into terraces for cultivation. South of the site thick river sand is met with in the wells or borings suggesting the existence of an old bed of the river Drishadvati. The depression demarcated by sand dunes on sides, runs along the Chautang Canal in a meandering way and is easily identifiable along Bhadra-Sothi alignment in Rajasthan.

The trench at Siswal measuring 2 m. sq. was sunk in the western part of the mound. It was dug to a maximum depth of 1.90 m. It yielded 1.25 m. thick habitational deposit above the natural soil, which consisted of yellow silt or alluvium containing a good quantity of *kankar* in the lower levels. In all, five habitational layers were discerned in the cutting.

On the basis of the pottery recovered from the excavations (fig. 18), the cultural sequence at the site is divided into two phases, A and B. Phase A, confined to layers (2) to (5), is characterised by the presence of Kalibangan I ware, including white paintings in addition to black over red and internally incised troughs. Phase B is distinguished by more evolved, rather sturdy, shapes, paucity of types and designs and the absence of the use of white pigment. This phase corresponds with Mitathal I. With this phase are perhaps to be associated a few Harappan shapes recovered from the surface of the mound.

Siswal has yielded all the characteristic fabrics of Kalibangan I culture from A to F (Lal and Thapar, 1965). In addition, a few sherds of coarse red ware and a single sherd of black-and-red ware were also recovered. The industry shows a clear trend of evolution in typology in the upper levels.

All pottery is wheel-made. Fabric A consists of medium to coarse red ware turned on slow wheel, potted irregularly, thin to medium in thickness, fired to grey or red core and painted with black or chocolate designs over matt red surfaces ranging from light red or yellowish to pinkish red colour. White pigment has been used in a number of designs as second colour to give a bichrome effect. The main shapes include vase with short everted, out-turned or out-curved rim, bowl with convex or tapering sides and featureless, flat or out-turned or everted rim, bowl or dish-on-stand, handled vase and perforated jar. The ware corresponds to Fabric A of Kalibangan I. Fabric B is a medium to thick red ware of medium fabric. It is well fired and its lower surface is rusticated, sometimes with finger marks producing parallel ridges. The ware corresponds to Fabric B of Kalibangan I. Fabric C, corresponding to C of Kalibangan I, is better potted and is treated with red slip, over which it is painted with black designs. Fabric D is characterized by a thick, sturdy, red, wheel-turned, well-fired pottery. The troughs are decorated with incised designs on the interior, as in Fabric D at Kalibangan. Fabrics E and F are rare at Siswal and cannot be distinguished from other fabrics but for the colour of the pots as at Kalibangan.

The finds collected from the surface of the site included terracotta triangular cakes, discs with tapering sides, oblong sling balls and beads and bangles painted with black pigment. A large saddle quern of stone, rubber stone and a wedge-shaped burnt brick constituted the other finds. No microlithic blades or copper objects were found.

The author has carried out explorations along the dry beds of the Sarasvati and Yamuna in Haryana (between lat. 28° 50′ and 30°. 50′ N and long. 74° 35′ and 77°.20′E), an archaeologically strategic area for understanding the matrix of prehistoric cultures of the Indo-Gangetic divide and the Ganga-Yamuna Doab. The explorations revealed 95 sites ranging between pre-Harappan and late Harappan periods. The Siswal wares were picked up at 48 sites in the above mentioned river valleys, covering an area from Sarangpur (Suraj Bhan, 1967), near Chandigarh, in the north to Tigrana near Bhiwani in the south and from Rukhi near Rohtak in the east to Bani near Sirsa in the west (fig. 20).

APPENDIX E

A NOTE ON THE EXCAVATION AT SAIPAI

B. B. Lal

Scholars have long been familiar with the occurrence of copper tools, commonly known as Copper Hoards, in the Ganga valley, with some extension to the south of that valley. At no place, however, were these tools found in a regular excavation. It has, therefore, always been a matter of debate as to what kind of pottery and other artefacts went along with the Hoard.

The excavation at Saipai in district Etawah, Uttar Pradesh, has placed, for the first time, these Hoards in a proper archaeological context, thus settling at least a part of the controversy, namely that relating to the pottery and other artefacts associated with them. The question about the ethnic identity of the Copper Hoard people may still be debated, although, no doubt, even in this connetion the cultural data supplied by the excavation will be of imense value.

Thus, when in August, 1969, the Archaeological Survery of India came to know that in the course of the ploughing up of a field near Saipai some copper tools had been found, Shri L. M. Wahal of the Northern Circle of the Survey was sent to the site to check on the news. He not only identified the tools as belonging to the Copper Hoard complex, but also studied the find-spot, which, as a result, was trial-trenched by him in May,1970. The trial-trench yielded, besides pottery, a hooked spearhead (fig. 22, no. 1). This made it amply clear that a further digging at the site would be rewarding.

Accordingly, in December, 1970, a small-scale excavation was taken up at the site, under the general direction of the present writer and with Shri Wahal as the principal supervisor. The work ended in February, 1971, the area excavated being 20 x 20 m.

As luck would have it, this excavation gave another tool of the Copper Hoard family. It was a harpoon encountered at a depth of 45 cm. below the surface (pl. IB; fig. 22, no. 3). The pottery that went along with it and was also found in the rest of the trench was a red ware. Many examples of it left the usual ochrous colour on the finger at the time of handling, as had been the case with the specimens from Hastinapura, Bisauli, Rajpur Parsu, etc. However, a study of the large number of pots, mostly fragmentary but sometimes complete, recovered from the excavation made it amply clear that many a pot had a red slip. In one case, even a design—criss-cross lines—was found painted in black colour. It would thus appear that the once-called Ochre Colour Ware may really have been black-on-red ware, the ochrous surface of some of the examples at Saipai and elsewhere being largely due to pulverisation through external causes. (Incidentally, would it be acceptable to scholars if this ware is now christened as Saipai Ware, for it is at this site for the first time that the ware has been found in actual association with a Capper Hoard ?).

From the point of view of typology, special attention is drawn by jars with flaring rim and bowls and basins sometimes having handles and/or spouts (pls. IIA and B, fig. 21, nos. 19-20). A fragment of a stem was suggestive of the dish-on-stand type, while in another case a ring-stand was indicated.

A very noteworthy feature of the Saipai ware is the occurrence of incised decorations on the exterior. The decorations include rows of dots or dashes or series of triangular compartments enclosing rows of dashes.

Amongst the other finds from the excavation, mention may be made of querns, mullers, pounders, pallets and balls of sandstone, a fragmentary blade of chert and a flake of chalcedony. Also found were some bones of the *Bos indicus*, whereby one would conclude the domestification of that animal.

As to the dwellings, no evidence was obtained by way of plans. However, the occurrence of lumps of clay bearing reed-impressions indicated some kind of wattle-and daub construction. A fragment of burnt earth with three faces smooth was suggestive of a brick, but surely much more evidence is needed before it can be said that the Copper Hoard people made their houses of kiln-burnt bricks.

In one of his earlier papers (Lal, 1951), the present writer demonstrated that the Copper Hoard people were unlikely to have been the Indo-Aryans. The evidence of pottery now encountered in definite association with the Copper Hoards at Saipai shows that these people are also different from the Harappans (this will remain the position until it can be demonstrated by evidence from intermediary sites that the Copper Hoard pottery is derived ultimately from the Harappan).

In the present state of our knowledge, therefore, it would appear once again that the Copper Hoard people were neither Aryans nor Harappans but of some other ethnic group, occupying the Ganga valley, with occasional intrusions into the regions to the south.

As to the date of this occupation, three different pieces of evidence may be invoked. In the first place, it is known that the Ochre Coloured Ware (which is the same as the Saipai Ware) ante-dated the Painted Grey Ware (Lal, 1954-55). Secondly, the occurrence of a fragment of an anthropomorphic figure at Lothal is suggestive of a date around 1900 B.C. (Lal, 1962-63; Gupta, 1965). And finally, below are given eight thermoluminiscence dates which the present writer has received through the courtesy of Professor S . Nurul Hasan. These were worked out by Dr. David Zimmerman of the Research Laboratory for Archaeology and History of Art, Oxford.

Site	*Sample No.*	*TL Age*
Atranjikhera	111-C1	2280 B.C.
"	111-C2	1250 B.C.

Lal-Qila	112-A1	1730 B.C.
,,	112-A2	2030 B.C.
Jhinjhana	113-B1	1570 B.C.
,,	113-B2	2650 B.C.
Nasirpur	114-A1	1500 B.C.
,,	114-A2	1180 B.C.

Of the foregoing dates, three are prior to 2000 B.C., three between 2000 B.C. and 1500 B.C. and only two after 1500 B.C.

From an overall assessment, therefore, it would appear that the Copper Hoard culture flourished in the first half of the second millennium B.C., if it did not have an earlier beginning. Working from a different angle, Gupta (1963) has also come to a similar conclusion.

APPENDIX F

THE OCHRE-COLOURED POTTERY—A GEOCHRONOLOGICAL STUDY

Dr. B. B. Lal

Ever since the Ochre-Coloured Pottery came to be recognised as a distinct industry of the Copper Hoard culture, many archaeologists have advanced the view that the worn and rolled appearance of the pottery is due to flooding and water-logging. This conclusion is based on a general and visual examination of the OCP horizons, and not on the results of careful structural and textural studies of the deposits in which this pottery is found. Although it has been reported (Gaur, 1969-2, p. 99) that soil specimens from OCP deposits from Atranjikhera were subjected to analysis, the results of the analysis have not been published. In view of the importance of this pottery, soil samples from OCP horizons exposed at Ahichchhatra, Bargaon, Hastinapura, Ṇasirpur and Jhinjhana were subjected to mechanical analysis by the author, since such a study was expected to throw light on the mechanism of transportation and deposition of the material constituting these strata. The results of these investigations, which have already been published (Dr. Lal, 1969), seemed to indicate the effect of wind on transportation and sedimentation of the material of the OCP strata. In view of this interesting observation, it was considered desirable to extend the investigation to some other OCP sites. Accordingly, soil specimens from OCP horizons exposed at Ambkheri and Atranjikhera have been analysed, and the specimens from Ahichchhatra, Bargaon, Hastinapura, Nasirpur and Jhinjhana have also been subjected to further analysis in extension of the work already reported (Dr. Lal, 1969).

Site	Specimen No.	Percentage of standard grades in mm.					
		Medium Sand 0.60-0.20	Fine Sand 0.20-0.06	Coarse Silt 0.06-0.02	Medium Silt 0.02-0.006	Fine Silt 0.006-0.002	Clay <0.002
Ahichchhatra	1	1	7	52	40	—	—
	2	—	10	40	50	—	—
	3	1	13	43	43	—	—
	4	1	2	33	76	3	5
	5	—	9	38	49	4	—
Ambkheri	1	2	38	30	30	—	—
	2	2	39	30	29	—	—
	3	2	37	31	30	—	—
	4	3	37	31	29	—	—
	5	1	26	54	19	—	—
Bargaon	1	1	21	39	39	—	—
	2	1	22	34	43	—	—
Hastinapura	1	1	26	41	31	1	—
	2	1	33	35	30	1	—
Nasirpur	1	3	43	23	27	4	—
	2	1	26	30	39	2	2
Jhinjhana	1(A_1)	1	20	30	44	3	2
	2(A_2)	1	7	47	40	3	2
	3(A_3)	—	12	33	50	3	2
	4(B_1)	1	22	40	32	5	—
	5(B_2)	1	16	38	41	4	—
	6(B_3)	1	12	37	50	–	—
	7(B_4)	—	3	28	69	–	—
	8(B_5)	—	3	24	73	—	—
	9(B_7)	—	6	64	26	4	—
Atranjikhera	1(3)	1	7	38	54	—	—
	2(4)	—	6	16	77	1	—
	3(5)	1	12	60	27	—	—
	4(6)	1	9	22	68	—	—
	5(7)	1	12	67	20	—	—
	6(11)	1	14	60	25	—	—
	7(17)	1	16	33	50	—	—

Statistical measures		Percentage of typical grades in mm.				
Median (Md)	Sorting. Coeff. (So)	0.01-0.07	0.01-0.10	0.06-0.006	0.06-0.002	<0.06
0.03	1.48	83	86	92	92	92
0.02	1.71	76	79	90	90	90
0.03	1.87	76	82	86	86	86
0.01	1.16	81	82	89	92	97
0.02	1.58	83	87	87	91	91
0.03	1.72	50	61	60	60	60
0.04	2.36	61	72	59	59	59
0.04	2.33	55	64	61	61	61
0.05	2.43	61	72	60	60	60
0.05	2.47	73	81	73	73	73
0.03	1.91	70	78	78	78	78
0.03	1.91	68	74	77	77	77
0.04	1.91	72	81	72	73	73
0.04	2.24	62	75	65	66	66
0.05	2.77	49	61	50	54	54
0.03	2.24	63	72	69	71	73
0.02	1.71	74	80	74	77	79
0.02	1.39	84	88	87	90	92
0.02	1.36	82	87	83	86	88
0.03	1.85	69	76	72	77	77
0.02	1.68	76	82	79	83	83
0.02	1.60	85	89	87	87	87
0.02	1.41	84	85	97	97	97
0.02	1.22	84	85	97	97	97
0.03	1.36	91	93	90	94	94
0.02	1.82	92	95	92	92	92
0.01	1.28	82	85	93	94	94
0.03	1.53	88	93	87	87	87
0.01	1.39	82	85	90	90	90
0.03	1.32	90	93	87	87	87
0.04	1.53	85	90	85	85	85
0.02	1.79	84	90	83	83	83

The method of mechanical analysis is the same as described earlier. For mechanical analysis, soil samples were air-dried and sieved through 0.20 mm. sieve. The sieved material was dispersed in distilled water and subjected to sedimentation analysis by the hydrometer method. In each case, 50 gm. of the sieved material was taken and dispersed so as to produce 1000 cc. of the suspension. No sample contained material coarser than 0.20 mm.

In the accompanying published table are shown the standard grades of grain sizes. The statistical measures, median (Md) and sorting coefficient (So), and the typical grades have also been worked out, as they give an idea of the force ef current, the range of velocity and the degree of turbulence of the transporting agent.

From the tabulated data it is observed that most of the specimens are free from the clay grade; only five specimens have been found to contain a small proportion of this grade. Three specimens from Jhinjhana and one specimen from Nasirpur show 2% of clay, and one specimen from Ahichchhatra contains clay to the extent of 5%. Medium sand is present to the extent of 1% - 3%. Since material coarser than 0.20 mm. is absent, the medium sand fraction falls in the grain size of 0.20 mm. The proportion of fine silt ranges from 1% to 5% and some specimens are altogether free from fine silt grade. These specimens are largely composed of fine sand, and coarse and medium silt.

The statistical measures of these specimens are very interesting. The mean average diameter (Md) of the five specimens from Ahichchhatra ranges from 0.01 mm. to 0.03 mm. Their sorting coefficient ranges from 1.16 to 1.87 and falls well below the limit (i.e., 2.50) indicating good sorting. All these specimens are, therefore, well-sorted.

The material from Ambkheri, however, shows different characteristics. In this case, the mean average diameter (Md) lies between 0.03 mm. and 0.05 mm. These deposits are distinctly coarser than those from Ahichchhatra. Moreover, their sorting coefficient varies from 2.33 to 2.47, and only one specimen shows a sorting coefficient of 1.72. These specimens are, therefore, not so well-sorted as those from Ahichchhatra.

The mean average diameter (Md) of the two specimens from Bargaon is 0.03 mm. Their sorting coefficient is 1.91, which falls much below the limit of 2.50 for well-sorted sediments. This value of the coefficient is slightly higher than what is shown by the deposits from Ahichchhatra. The material from Bargaon, however, shows a better sorting than the specimens from Ambkheri. The specimens from Hastinapura present a similar picture with mean average diameter of 0.04 mm. and a sorting coefficient varying between 1.91 and 2.24. The two specimens from Nasirpur have a mean average diameter of 0.03 mm.-0.05 mm. and their sorting coefficient varies from 2.24 to 2.77. The material thus shows rather poor sorting.

Of the nine specimens from Jhinjhana, seven show a mean average diameter of 0.02 mm.; only two specimens have a mean average diameter of 0.03 mm. Their sorting coefficient ranges from 1.22 to 1.85 and is thus much below the limit of 2.50 for well-sorted sediments. The seven specimens from Atranjikhera show almost similar characteristics. Their mean average diameter lies in the range 0.01 mm. - 0.03 mm.; only one specimen shows a mean average diameter of 0.04 mm. The sorting coefficient varies from 1.28 to 1.82. All these specimens are characterised by marked sorting.

The typical grades present in all these samples may now be discussed. The grades have been worked out with a view to studying the effect of transportation by water and wind. It may be observed here that loessic material or wind-blown dust falls in the grade 0.01 mm. - 0.07 mm. If any stuctureless homogeneous scdiment is found to contain 70% - 80% of the material in this grade, it falls in the category of wind-laid loessic deposits. Fine sand and coarse and medium silt (0.01 mm.-0.10 mm.) can be transported by wind over long distances. In fact, strong winds can transport coarse and medium silt (0.06 mm.-0.006 mm.) by suspension. The presence of 80% of the material in the coarse, medium and fine silt grades (0.06 mm.-0.002 mm.) indicates wind action, and material so deposited is wind-borne loess. Further, if 70%-90% of the material falls in the silt and clay grades only (<0.06 mm.), the deposit is wind-borne silt. Again, a sediment which contains 87% - 99.5% of the material in the fine sand, silt and clay grades (<0.20 mm.), is wind-borne silt. Coarser material falling in the grade 0.20 mm. - 0.06 mm. cannot be air-borne, but it can be transported by wind in short leaps only. All these criteria are helpful in determining the mechanism of transportation and sedimentation of the OCP–bearing deposits.

The five specimens from Ahichchhatra show that the typical grade of grain size, 0.01 mm. - 0.07 mm., accounts for 76%—83% of the material of each specimen, and the next typical grade (i.e., 0.01 mm. - 0.10 mm.) is present to the extent of 79%—87%. The material falllng in the coarse and medium silt grades (0.06 mm. - 0.02 mm. and 0.02 mm. - 0.006 mm.) is present to the extent of 86%—92%. When the other typical grades are taken into account, it is seen that the fractions falling in the grade 0.06 mm. - 0.002 mm., and in the grade smaller than 0.06 mm. account for 86% - 92% and, 86% - 97% respectively. Their size-frequency curves fall in the fine sand and coarse and medium silt range and show elongated S-shaped patterns typical of eolian dust. There is thus reason to believe that the deposits are eolian and that the strata were formed as a result of wind activity.

When the typical grades in the specimens from Ambkheri are considered, it is seen that the grade 0.01 mm. - 0.07 mm. accounts for 50% - 73% of the material. The next typical grade, 0.01 mm. - 0.10 mm., is present to the extent of 61% - 72%; only one specimen shows 81% of the material in this grade. Thc coarse and medium silt grades (i.e., 0.06 mm. - 0.02 mm. and 0.02 m. - 0.006 mm.) account for 59% - 73%. These deposits thus do not appear to fall in the category of Ahichchhatra specimens. The marked difference between the deposits from these two sites is clearly brought out by the cumulative curves. As pointed out earlier, the specimens from Ahichchhatra show elongated S-shaped size-frequency curves, but those from Ambkheri give generally straight curves without any pronounced inflexion. Similarly, the size-frequency curves of the specimens from Bargaon, Hastinapura and Nasirpur are markedly different from those of Ahichchhatra specimens. The cumulative curves of specimens from Jhinjhana are typical elongated S-shaped curves similar to those exhibited by the specimens from Ahichchhatra.

Further, from the study of typical grades it is seen that the material from Atranjikhera is similar to that from Ahichchhatra. Five specimens (1-5) contain more than 80% of the material in the grade 0.01 mm. - 0.07 mm. Similarly, the grade 0.01 mm. - 0.10 mm. shows a very high percentage ranging from 85% to 95%. Specimen 6(11) shows 93% of the material in the grade 0.01 mm. - 0.10 mm. and 90% in the grade 0.01 mm. - 0.07 mm. Similar features are exhibited by specimen 7 (17) which has 84% of the material in the grade 0.01 mm. - 0.07 mm., and 90% in the grade 0.01 mm. —0.10 mm.

It would be seen that the percentage of coarse and medium silt (i.e., 0.06. mm.— 0.006 mm.) is generally very high in the specimens from Ahichchhatra, Jhinjhana and Atranjikhera. Similar is the case with the grade 0.01 mm. - 0.10 mm. Of the total number of twentyone specimens from these three sites, as many as eighteen contain more than 80% of the material in the grade 0.06 mm. - 0.006 mm., and show marked sorting in the coarse-medium silt grade. Similarly, nineteen specimens show more than 80% of the material in the grade 0.01 mm. - 0.10 mm. The specimens from Ambkheri, Bargaon, Hastinapura and Nasirpur, however, do not show this degree of sorting in any of the two grades in question. The specimens from Bargaon and Hastinapura can thus be placed in one category, whereas those from Ambkheri and Nasirpur seem to fall in another group with a distinctly higher coefficient of sorting.

It would be noticed that the specimens from all these sites do not represent a flood loam or alluvium in situ. Fluviatile deposits contain all the grades, sand, silt and clay, in varying proportions, but the specimens under discussion are highly sorted. The clay grade is either present in a very low proportion or is altogether absent. In fact, no clay is present in the specimens from Ambkheri, Bargaon and Hastinapura. Further, all the specimens are free from coarse sand. The proportion of medium sand also is very small, generally 1%. and only four specimen from Ambkheri and one specimen from Nasirpur contain 2% - 3% of this grade. There is thus unmistakable evidence of the effect of transportation on the concentration and sorting of the material under examination

It is well known that fluviatile deposits show bedding planes, being stratified, and all the grades, such as sand, silt and clay, are present in varying proportions. The OCP horizons exposed at these sites, however, do not show any detectable stratification or bedding planes. They are neither current-bedded nor ripple-marked, but represent megascopically structureless homogeneous deposits. In view of these features, the OCP strata do not appear to have been deposited by water. Since no coarse material is present, it is reasonable to conclude that the environment of deposition was neither turbulent nor rough. Quiet water environmeut, which characterises water-logging, favours the sedimentation of laminated material and these laminations are produced only in the absence of turbulence at the bottom. In view of these considerations, the deposits in question cannot be attributed to flooding and water-logging.

How then were the deposits coustituting the OCP strata formed ? The marked sorting of the material and freedom from stratification and bedding planes would appear to rule out the possibility of fluviatile origin of the sediments. If the sherds were transported from a distance during floods and deposited at the site of Atranjikhera, as has been stated by Gaur (Gaur, 1969-2, p. 95), the material of the OCP horizon should have been coarse, but even coarse sand is absent. Moreover, if the site had experienced water-logging, as postulated, again by Gaur (Gaur, 1965-1, p. 142), the deposits should have been laminated. Actually the OCP horizons at Atranjikhera and other sites, viz. Jhinjhana, Bargaon, Ambkheri, Nasirpur and Ahichchhatra, have been found to be megascopically structureless and homogeneons, without any signs of lamination or stratification. The possibility of stagnant water shedding its fine, suspended load without producing laminated deposits cannot be visualised, as sedimentation under these conditions shows a degree of stratificaticn and gives rise to megascopically detectable laminations. In view of the freedom of tho OCP strata from bedding planes, current-bedding and ripple-marks and the excellent sorting of the material, it seems probable that the deposits were formed on account of wind activity. Wind-laid sediments, such as eolian dusts or loesses, are free from laminations, are highly sorted and contain more then 80% of the material in the grade 0.01 mm. - 0.10 mm. Eolian dust is generally calcareous and the presence of lime in most of the specimens is thus significant. It appears that the OCP strata were formed by the sedimentation of wind-blown dust. Whereas Ambkheri and Nasirpur have shown a good proportion of wind-blown dust, and Bargaon and Hastinapura have yielded a high percentage of wind - borne material, aeolion silt is a dominant component of the deposits from Ahichchhatra,

Jhinjhana and Atranjikhera In fact, aeolion silts predominate to such an extent that the climate must have been drier than at present. The study of deposits from several sites in Gujrat has revealed a remarkable preponderance of wind-laid material, similar to the aeolion deposits of Europe and Africa. The results of this study need not be discussed here. Suffice it to say that the agreement in textural characteristics between the material from OCP deposits on the one hand and the wind-blown silts from Gujrat and the loessic deposits from Europe and Africa on the other is so close that the aeolion origin of the former canot be doubted. The random distribution of the sherds at different levels within the OCP horizons could thus be visualised as being due to continuous sedimentation of wind-blown material at the sites when the OCP was being used.

The OCP occurs in a worn and weathered condition. It has generally been described as rolled, worn and ill-fired with a friable and powdery surface and a thick fabric. The worn and rolled appearance of the sherds, their weathered surface and the pealing off of the slipped surface, have generally been attributed to insufficient firing, flooding and water-logging. Contact with river silt has also been considered to be responsibile for their weathering. In fact, Gaur has stated that the OCP horizon at Atranjikhera had been flooded and remained water-logged for a considerable time (Gaur, 1967, p. 47). According to him the OCP sherds were probably transported by flood waters and deposited in the depressions away from the place of regular habitation (Gaur, 1969-2, p. 95). This view appears to be untenable, since none of the soil specimens from the OCP horizon represents a flood loam, which generally contains material of all the grades from coarse sand to clay. The matrix, in which the OCP was found embedded, is completely free from material corresponding in size and coarseness to the sherds; and selective or preferential transportation of sherds by the flood waters to the total exclusion of gravel and coarse sand was out of the question.

It is important to observe that weathering is not peculiar to this particular ware; other pottery has also been found in a weathered condition with worn surface and rounded edges. For instance, Alamgirpur I has yielded weathered pottery. Similarly, ochre-washed pottery in rolled and weathered condition has been reported from Nasik I. The various aspects of the problem of weathering of the OCP merit a careful investigation. The three main factors, which are said to be responsible for the weathered appearance of this pottery, are firing, flooding and water-logging, and the action of the river silt. These may now be considered.

Firing:

Inadequacy of firing has been considered to be responsible for the worn and weathered surface of the OCP. This theory, however, does not seem to have been substantiated by scientific tests. The OCP is generally red and ochre-coloured; occasionally the core is grey. The observed friability is superficial. In fact, this pottery is characterised by a fine texture indicating the use of a levigated clay, such as is generally associated with other wares. The red colour of the pottery indicates the presence of ferric oxide and the amount of ferrous oxide has been found to be inappreciable. There is thus evidence to indicate that this pottery has been fired well at a sufficiently high temperature in an oxidizing atmosphere. In this connection it is pertinent to remark that the weathering of well-fired bricks and pottery is neither unusual nor uncommon. In view of these considerations, the inadequacy of firing as a factor of weathering has to be ruled out.

Flooding aud Water-logging:

Although the weathered and worn condition of this pottery has been attributed to flooding and water-logging, no evidence has been put forward to substantiate thls view. If the weathering were due to flooding and water-logging, many wares would have exhibited the sort of weathering noticed in OCP. However, it is on record that at Bargaon, where the OCP and another red pottery have been found together (Deshpande, 1967-3), the latter does not show any effect of weathering. It is difficult to explain why the OCP has been affected by flooding and water-logging, whereas the associated pottery has escaped rolling. The phenomenon of weathering noticed in the OCP has, therefore, to be attributed to some factor other than flooding and water-logging. It is well known that unweathered pottery and bricks have been found at Harappa and Mohenjodaro, where the water table was high enough to expose them to the action of sub-soil moisture. The finds from these levels, however, did not exhibit any weathering. It is clear that the explanation for the weathering of the OCP must be sought elsewhere.

Effect of River-silt :

It has been suggested by many workers that the OCP became worn and weathered due to abrasion with river silt. A careful examination of the pottery leaves no doubt that only the broken edges of the sherds present a weathered and rounded appearance, and that the body of the ware shows little rounding effect. The pottery, which is transported over long distances by river currents, suffers considerable weathering and erosion all over the surface including the edges. In view of these considerations, it is difficult to visualise how the river-silt could have brought about the weathering of the OCP and rounded off the edges only.

Cause of Weathering:

From the above it would be seen that the conditions of firing were such as could produce a compact ware of usual hardness. It is further evident that the firing of the pottery took place under oxidizing conditions, as much of the iron oxide is present in the ferric state and the amount of ferrous oxide is inappreciable. The weathering of the OCP, therefore, cannot be attributed to inadequate firing. As already observed, the well-burnt Harappa pottery from the lowest levels saturated with subsoil water is strong and hard with a fresh slipped surface, bearing clear, painted designs, This pottery, however, suffers rapid disintegration and weathering, if exposed to air without washing. The reason for the weathering is obvious. Throughout the long period of inhumation in the soil, the pottery remained in contact with subsoil moisture containing soluble salts. In course of time an equilibrium was established between the pottery and its saline and moist environment; and in the condition of equalibrium the pottery remained free from weathering. Soon after excavation, the moisture present in the pottery evaporated rapidly leaving the crystallized salts in the body of the pottery. The crystallization of the soluble salts in the changed environment brought about the disintegration of the pottery.

Soil analysis data discussed earlier have established the absence of flood deposits and fluviatile sediments in the OCP horizons. Similarly, river-silt has been found to be absent, since no stratified deposits have been encountered. Laminated clay deposits, which are formed under quiet water environment during water-logging, have also been found to be absent. The mechanical analysis data clearly demonstrate a distinct wind activity indicating arid conditions. In view of these considerations the author is led to the conclusion that the OCP remained exposed to atmosphere for a considerable period; and that before the OCP strata at various sites were underlaid by later deposits. the pottery suffered weathering as a result of considerable exposure. It is, therefore, not improbable that when the OCP people were living, there was a gradual deposition of wind-blown material under arid conditions and the pottery became weathered. Such a mechanism of transportation and sedimentation of the material constituting the matrix of the OCP horizons would also explain the random distribution of the pottery.*

*The author's profuse thanks are due to his colleague Shri D. S. Srivastava for supplying the mechanical analysis data presented in this paper.

APPENDIX G

TECHNICAL NOTES ON NBP WARE

Extract from "Ancient India", No. 1, New Delhi, 1946, p.58.

"1. The black coating contains about 13% ferrous oxide which is responsible for the black shade. The original slip was evidently a highly ferruginous body (possibly consisting of a finely levigated mixture of clay and red ochre) ground in water and applied to the surface of the vessel before it was fired. The black colour was doubtlessly developed by the action of reducing gases formed in the kiln. The polishing might have been done before or after the firing. The coating is not a siliceous glaze.

2. The black polished film has been analysed with the following results:-

Silica, 46.55%; ferrous oxide, 25.20%; alumina, 15.33%; lime, 4.74%; magnesia, 3.43%; water, (110°C), 3.45%; alkalies not determined.

Fragments of black pottery were heated in air over a bunsen burner with the result that they lost their black colour and gradually became light red. These fragments were again heated strongly in a glass tube while carbon monoxide was passed over them. This treatment changed their colour to black again. We have also succeeded in converting ordinary red and white pottery into black by heating with pieces of wood. There is no doubt therefore that the black colour is produced under reducing conditions and the red one under oxiding ones in kiln. Although Lucas has tried to prove that the black colour of pottery is due only to carbon, yet our experiments leave no doubt that ferrous silicate is also produced. Since ferrous silicate is said to be of blue black colour, its share in colouring the body black is obvious. The presence of lime and magnesia further indicates that compound ferrous-lime and ferrous-magnesia silicate are also probably formed, which bring about the fusion of the black film in the course of burning. That should account for the high polish and hardness of the surfacc of some of these specimens. I agree with Lucas that carbon is deposited in the pores of the pottery when a smoky atmosphere is created in the kiln by means of organic matter, but it is obvious that some tany matter will also be produced and deposited in the pottery to enhance its black colour."

Mohd. Sana Ullah

Extracts from 'The Surface Treatment of Early Indian Pottery, "Man", 1953, Art. 58, pp. 41-42.

"Recent study of a large collection of sherds of Indian pottery of the neolithic/megalithic and early historical periods has led me to formulate a theory concerning the method by which their surfaces were treated, which I would like to propose. It seems likely that this method is actually far commoner than any other in the pre-glaze stages of ceramic technology, and it has not so far been recognised."

"Though in some cases of carefully thrown pottery of the proto-historic period from the Deccan the surface dressing has been washed as a suspension of finely ground haematite before firing, the greater part of early Indian pottery has been burnished, or as it is often called, 'polished'. Burnishing of pots is common at all times in many parts of the world, but on the Indian sherds that I examined the individual slight facets imparted to the surface of the body by the burnishing in the green-hard state were exactly co-extensive with the slight streaks visible in the colour layer. It is, therefore, probable that the facets and the streaks were imparted by the same strokes; that is that the burnishing and colouring agent were the same. I conclude that haematite dressing was rubbed on to the surface with a knob of softish ochre, like those found at Tell-ed-Duweir."

"The pot was probably centred on the wheel in its green-hard state, and the haematite knob was held against it as it revolved. If once this method of applying haematite as a surface dressing for Indian pottery is accepted as fundamental, all the varieties of early wares can be accounted for by variation in firing techniques. The variation of colour in oxidized wares can be explained by the variation of the temperatures at which they were fired, since the red colour of haematite in firing changes progressively between about 600°C and 850°C. The grey-bodied wares can likewise be accounted for by firing under special reducing conditions. It is probable that the grey wares of the Ganges valley sites were fired in open saggars (refractory clay boxes) stacked one above the other in the kiln. The ware in saggars closed by a saggar above them would fire in a fully reducing atmosphere, whilst the ware in the top saggar, which would be open, would fire in an oxidizing atmosphere, and thus come from the kiln red. The hypothesis is borne out by the presence on the Ganges sites of a small proportion of red ware of the same form and fabric as grey. In view of the close association on the sites of the Northern Black Polished ware with the grey wares, and of what was proposed above concerning the method of applying haematite dressing, the Northern Black Polished ware can be explained as a haematite-dressed ware, saggar-fired."

"The vitreous effect found on the surface of the finer early Indian wares can be accounted for, on the hypothesis of haematite dressing, by the action of the ferric oxide in firing as a flux to that part of the body clay in immediate contact with it, which would result in the formation of a vitrified skin at quite a low temperature. The skin would tend to separate itself from the more granular body, and result in the familiar flaking of the surface of worn or damaged pottery."

P. S. Rawson

Extract from "Indian Archaeology—A Review", 1955-56 pp. 56-57.

"Several specimens of the Northern Black Polished Ware were examined for colour-development and changes in the clay on baking with a view to determining the conditions of its firing and the technique of its fabrication. This investigation led to a new observation, viz., the development on heating of spherulites on the surface of the shining layer of the Ware. The lustre on the surface of the Ware therefore appears to be composed of some easily-fusible material, possibly of organic origin, which undergoes incipient fusion at a low heat. The layer just below the uppermost film was, in most cases, noticed to be buff or orange-yellow. The blackening of the uppermost surface may, therefore, be due to some sort of post-firing treatment, in which the pottery, still hot from the kiln, was coated with some liquid such as a oil, juice of some plant or a similar organic concoction. Natural resins such as shellac or benzoin, vegetable or animal fat, iron-rich organic musilage, such as plantain- or *amla*-pulp or some similar organic material may have also been responsible for the production of the lustre. Further research is in progress. A systematic plan for the investigation of problems of ceramic archaeology was chalked out and experimental work initiated on such aspects as temperature-control under firing, colour change, pyrometry, density, hardness determination and ceramic petrography. The investigation is still in an experimental stage."

Dr. B. B. Lal

Extract from "Indian Archaeology-A Review", 1959-60, pp. 120-21.

"Attempts were made to synthesize the Northern Black Polished Ware in laboratory under carefully-controlled condilions, employing materials of definitely-known composition and firing at different temperatures. The investigation corroborated the already-published results (*1955-56*, p. 56) on the composition and technique of the Ware, though the exact conditions of firing and the nature of the ferruginous material employed in its manufacture still remained elusive."

Dr. B. B Lal

Extract from R.E.M. Wheeler's "Ealry India and Pakistan", London, 1959, p. 30.

"Many sites in northern and central India, occasionally as far south as Amaravati, have produced this Iron Age ware, which is as distinctive in the subcontinent as is *terra sigillata* on European sites. It is wheel-made and normally thin, with a highly lustrous surface ranging from grey or brown to black, and steel-like in quality. The paste is well levigated and is white to reddish. The bright gloss is not a glaze or lacquer. The process of manufacture is doubtful: it has been thought that after being turned on the wheel, the pots were subjected to elaborate burnishing, and then coated with a finely levigated, highly ferruginous clay, and again burnished; and that they were then fired under reducing conditions to a temperature producing an incipient fusion of the slip, this accounting for their exceptional hardness and lustre. Recently, the laboratory of the British Museum has questioned the burnishing without, as yet, providing any complete alternative explanation. Its present verdict is that the unfired pots were dipped in a suspension of a ferruginous inorganic material, probably resembling a red earth; and that, after firing to a temperature of c. 800° C., the kiln was sealed so that the pots cooled in a reducing atmosphere. The mineralogical identity of the "red earth" has not been discovered, and the main problem, namely the precise nature of the surface layer, still remains unsolved."

Miss Bimson, British Museum

Extract from "Current Science", December 20, 1966, 35, No. 24, p. 623.

"An analytical study of the lustrous coal black slip of the Ware indicated that the presence of magnetic oxide of iron is responsible for its black colour, and the formation of glass-like soda-alumina-silicate is responsible for its lustre.

An electron microscopic study of this slip has now confirmed the above analytical study. The shining coal black slip of the N.B.P. Ware consists of euhedral crystals of magnetic oxide or iron on a background of amorphous, structure-less, glass like material. Magnetic oxide or iron, $Fe'' F_2''2o_4$ is opaque, isometric and black with metallic lustre in reflected light."

K.T.M. Hegde

Abstracted from 'Some Technical Observations on, N. B. P. Ware Slip', "Potteries in Ancient India," Patna, 1969, pp. 188-92.

The earlier tests and examinations were duly taken into account and further examinations carried out on the N.B.P. slip. "On the basis of these examinations and investigations, we may tentatively suggest that black colour of the slip is materially on account of carbon and our experiments and observations do not substantiate the presence of magnetic or ferrous silicate.

Views of Lal mentioning the use of organic material which will deposit carbon on charring need attention. However, in view of the presence of a detachable clayey slip, post-firing application of organic liquids looks doubtful. The slip might have been obtained by the application of well levigated emulsion of refined clay and organic liquids (say, plant juices) over the dried pots. After the slip was dry, the pots were fired under reducing condition. The organic matter in the slip carbonized, without burning out, resulting in a uniform lustrous black surface."

H. C. Bhardwaj

Extracts from 'Physics and Chemistry in Indian Archaeology', paper read at the annual conference, Indian Archaeological Society, Nagpur, 1970.

"An analytical study of the lustrous coal black slip of the ware indicates (Hegde, 1962) a very high percentage of Sodium and iron in the slip. When heated in an open crucible the colour of the ware first turned yellow and finally red. When a very small fragment of the slip was held near a magnet it was attracted by the magnet, while a similar fragment of the body was found to be relatively less magnetic.

From the analytical data above, it was observed that the shiny black slip of the N.B.P. Ware was produced by an application of liquid clay, quite similar to that employed for preparing the body of the ware, but which in addition to levigation was carefully further sifted and cleaned for reducing heavier particles. This clear clay suspension was peptized by the addition of an alkaline material.

Peptized clay liquids give a black shine slip when fired in reducing condition on account of the following reaction taking place within the sealed kiln.

$3\ Fe_2^\circ 3$ plus Co $-2\ Fe_3^\circ 4$ plus Co_2

On the surface of the ware is, hence, produced a thin layer of black magnetic oxide of iron which is responsible for the black colour of the slip.

The effect of alkali is reduction of refractoriness or vitrification temperature of the clay. Alkali combines with alumina and silica in the clay to fuse them at as low a temperature as 70 C and hence acts like a flux.

The liquid so formed does not crystallize on cooling, instead forms an amorphous glass-like substance. This glass-like substance imparts the NBP a glossy lustrous surface finish."

"In the production of N.B.P. Ware slip, clay suspension was quite likely treated with a clear solution of 'Sajjimatti'. On heating the slipped pottery to 700° C. the Sodium components are decomposed to Soda which fluxes the clay to form complex silicates which on cooling impart the glaze, like glass, on the surface of the Ware."

K.T.M. Hegde

APPENDIX H

BIBLIOGRAPHY OF OCP AND RELATED LITERATURE

(The following bibliography prepared jointly by Shri K. N. Dikshit, Shri Shanker Nath and Editor, comprises literature on the OCP, but its scope had to be extended to include such related literature, where connection with the OCP has been indicated directly or indirectly. Ed.)

1. Agrawal, D.P., 1967-68: 'Protohistoric Chronology and Technological and Ecological Factors–A Synthesis', *Puratattva*, No. 1, Varanasi, pp. 17-23.

2. Agrawal, D.P., 1969-70: 'The Metal Technology of the Indian Protohistoric Cultures: Its Archaeological Implications', *Puratattva*, No. 3, Varanasi, pp. 15-22.

3. Agrawal, D.P., 1971: *The Copper Bronze Age in India*, New Delhi.

4. Agrawala, R.C., 1967: Brief report of excavation by R.C. Agrawala in collaboration with Prof J. Le Roy Davidson of California University at Noh, district Bharatpur, *Indian Archaeology-A Review*, 1963-64, New Delhi, pp. 28-29.

5. Allchin, Bridget and Raymond, 1968: '*The Birth of Indian Civilization*,' Bungay, England, pp. 200-206.

6. Bajpai, K.D., 1969-1: Comments by K.D. Bajpai on K. N. Dikshit's paper on the 'Nature of Harappan Wares in Sutlej Valley', *Potteries in Ancient India*, Patna, p. 68.

7. Bajpai, K.D., 1969-2: Comments by K.D. Bajpai on R.C. Gaur's paper on 'The Ochre Coloured Pottery, from Atranjikhera and its Significance', *Potteries in Ancient India*, Patna, p. 100.

8. Banerjee, N.R., 1969-1: Brief report of excavation by N.R. Banerjee at Ahichchhatra, *Indian Archaeology- A Review*, 1964-65, New Delhi, pp. 39-42.

9. Banerjee, N.R., 1969-2: Brief report of explorations by N.R. Banerjee at Bholni, Budhakhera, Janipur, Khatauli, Mandowala, Pajrana and Taharpur, district Saharanpur, *Indian Archaeology-A Review*, 1964-65, New Delhi, pp. 43-44.

10. Bongard-Levin, G.M., 1971: *Studies in Ancient India and Central Asia*, Calcutta, pp. 3-20 (being mostly English translation of part of No. 11 in this Biblography).

11. Bongard-Levin, G.M. and Deopik, D.V., 1957: 'K. probleme proiskhozhdeniya Narodov Munda (V suete arkheologicheskhikh issledovanic poslednikh let)', *Sovetskaya Ethnografiya*, no. 1, 1957, pp. 46-56.

12. Deshpande, M.N., 1959: Brief report of excavations at Daimabad, district, Ahmednagar, by M.N. Deshpande, *Indian Archaeology - A Review*, 1958-59, New Delhi, pp. 15-18.

13. Deshpande, M.N., 1965-1: Comments by M.N. Deshpande on A.Ghosh's paper on 'The Indus Civilization: its Origins, Authors, Extent and Chronology', *Indian Prehistory*: *1964*, Poona, pp. 127-29.

14. Deshpande, M.N. 1965-2: Brief report of explorations by M.N. Deshpande at Sikerera, district Muzaffarnagar, *Indian Archaeology- A Review*, 1962-63, New Delhi, pp. 36-37.

15. Deshpande, M.N., 1965-66 (under publication) Brief report of explorations by M. N. Deshpande at Aneki, Garh Qutubpur, Hetampur, Mayapur, Nasirpur, Puranpur, Salempur Mahdud, Sati Kund and Teliwala, district Saharanpur, *Indian Archaeology - A Review*, 1965-66.

16. Deshpande, M.N., 1967-1: Brief report of explorations by M.N. Deshpande at Gadharona, Sikri, Ambkheri, Shikarpur and Thataula (Khempur Kalera), district Saharanpur, *Indian Archaeology-A Review*, 1963-64, New Delhi, pp. 53-54.

17. Deshpande, M.N., 1967-2: Brief report of excavation by M.N, Deshpande at Ambkheri, *Indian Archaeology - A Review*, 1963-64, New Delhi, p. 56.

18, Deshpande, M.N., 1967-3: Brief report of excavation by M.N. Deshpande at Bargaon, *Indian Archaeology-A Review*, 1963-64, New Delhi, pp. 56-57.

19. Deshpande, M.N., 1969-1: Comments by M.N. Deshpande on Krishna Deva's paper on the 'Problem of the Ochre-Coloured Pottery', *Potteries in Ancient India*, Patna, pp. 79-80.

20. Deshpande, M.N., 1969-2: Comments by M. N. Deshpande on R.C. Gaur's paper on 'The Ochre-Coloured Pottery from Atranjikhera and its Significance', *Potteries in Ancient India*, Patna, p. 100.

21. Deshpande, M.N., 1969-3: Comments by M.N. Deshpande on K.N. Dikshit's paper on the 'Nature of Harappan Wares in Sutlej Valley', *Potteries in Ancient India*, Patna, p. 65.

22. Deshpande, M.N., 1971: 'Archaeological Sources for the Reconstruction of the History of Sciences of India', *Indian Journal of History of Science*, No. 1, Vol. 6, p. 14.

23. Deva. K., 1969-1: 'Problem of the Ochre-Coloured Pottery', *Potteries in Ancient India*, Patna, 1969, pp. 75-82 (including comments by others).

24. Deva, K., 1969-2: Comments by K. Deva on K.N. Dikshit's paper on the 'Nature of Harappan Wares in Sutlej Valley', *Potteries in Ancient India*, Patna, p. 65.

25. Deva, K., 1969-3: Comments by K. Deva on R.C. Gaur's paper on the 'Ochre-Coloured Pottery from Atranjikhera and its Significance', *Potteries in Ancient India*, Patna, p. 100.

26. Dikshit, K.N., 1967-1: 'Harappa Culture and its Aftermath' *Archaeocivilization*, Nos. 3–4, Paris.

27. Dikshit, K.N., 1967-2: 'Exploration along the right bank of river Sutlej in Punjab', *Journal of Indian History*, Vol. XLV, Part II.

28. Dikshit, K.N., 1968: 'The Copper Hoards in the light of recent discoveries', *Bulletin of Ancient Indian History and Archaeology*, University of Saugor, 2, pp. 43-50.

29. Dikshit, K.N., 1969-1: 'Nature of Harappan Wares in Sutlej Valley' *Potteries in Ancient India*, Patna, pp. 56-66 (including comments by others).

30. Dikshit, K.N., 1969-2: Comments by K.N. Dikshit on R.C. Gaur's paper on 'The Ochre-Coloured Pottery from Atranjikhera and its Significance', *Potteries in Ancient India*. Patna, p. 101.

31. Dikshit, K.N. 1970: 'Harappa Culture in Western Uttar Pradesh', *Bulletin of the National Museum*, No. 2, New Delhi, pp. 21-28.

32. Dikshit, K N. and Narain, H.K., 1967: Brief report of exploration at Kat-palon, district Jullunder, by K.N. Dikshit and H.K. Narain, *Indian Archaeology- A Review*, 1963-64, New Delhi, p. 28.

33. Gaur, R.C . 1965-1: Comments by R.C. Gaur on A. Ghosh's paper on the 'Indus Civilization: Its Origins, Authors, Extent and Chronology', *Indian Prehistory: 1964*, Poona, pp. 142-45.

34. Gaur, R.C., 1965-2: Comments by R.C. Gaur on B.K. Thapar's paper on the 'Relationship of the Indian Chalcolithic Cultures with West Asia', *Indian Prehistory: 1964*, Poona, p. 167.

35. Gaur, R.C., 1965-3 Comments by R.C. Gaur on H.D. Sankalia's paper on the 'Traditional Indian Chronology

and C^{14} dates of Excavated Sites', *Indian Prehistory: 1964*, Poona, p. 231.

36. Gaur, R.C., 1965-4: Brief report of excavations by R.C. Gaur at Atranjikhera, *Indian Archaeology-A Review*, 1962-63, New Delhi, pp. 34-36.

37. Gaur, R.C., 1965-66: (under publication) Brief report of continued excavation by R.C. Gaur at Atranjikhera, *Indian Archaeology-A Review*, 1965-66.

38. Gaur, R.C., 1967: Brief report of excavations by R C. Gaur at Atranjikhera, *Indian Archaeology- A Review*, 1963-64, New Delhi, pp. 45-49.

39. Gaur, R.C., 1968: Brief report of excavations by R.C. Gaur at Atranjikhera, *Indian Archaeology - A Review*, 1967-68, New Delhi, pp. 45-46.

40. Gaur, R.C., 1969-1: Comments by R.C. Gaur on K.N.Dikshit's paper on the 'Nature of Harappan Wares in Sutlej Valley', *Potteries in Ancient India*, Patna, p. 66.

41. Gaur, R.C., 1969-2: 'The Ochre-Coloured Pottery from Atranjikhera and its Significance', *Potteries in Ancient India*, Patna, pp. 95-101 (including comments by others).

42. Gaur, R.C., 1970-71: 'An Appraisal of the Proto-historic Problems of the Ganga-Yamuna Doab', *Puratattva*, No. 4, New Delhi, pp. 42-50.

43. Gaur, R.C., and Hasan, S. Nurul, 1964: *Excavations at Atranjikhera, 1964* (A cyclostyled preliminary report, informally circulated).

44. Ghosh, A., 1965: 'The Indus Civilization: Its Origins, Authors, Extent and Chronology', *Indian Prehistory:1964*, Poona, pp. 113-54 (including comments by others).

45. Gupta, S.P., 1963: 'The Indian Copper Hoards: The Problems of Homogeneity, Stages of Development, Origin, Authorship and Dating', *Journal of the Bihar Research Society*, Vol. XLIX, Parts I and IV, Patna, pp. 147-66.

46. Gupta, S.P., 1965-1: 'Further Copper Hoards: a reassessment in the light of new evidence', *Journal of the Bihar Research Society*, Vol. LI, Parts I and IV, Patna, pp. 1-7.

47. Gupta, S.P., 1965-2: Comments by S.P. Gupta on A. Ghosh's paper on 'The Indus Civilization: Its Origins, Authors, Extent and Chronology', *Indian Prehistory: 1964*, Poona, pp. 146-47.

48. Gupta, S.P., 1969-1: Comments by S.P. Gupta on K.N. Dikshit's paper on the 'Nature of Harappan Wares in Sutlej Valley', *Potteries in Ancient India*, Patna, p. 66.

49. Gupta, S.P., 1969-2: Comments by S.P. Gupta on Krishna Deva's paper on the 'Problem of Ochre-Coloured Pottery', *Potteries in Ancient India*, Patna, p. 81.

50. Gupta, S.P., 1969-3: Comments by S.P. Gupta on R.C. Gaur's paper on 'The Ochre-Coloured Pottery from Atranjikhera and its Significance', *Potteries in Ancient India*, Patna, p. 101.

51. Handa, Devendra, 1968: 'Harappans, Ochre Ware and the Copper Hoards', *East and West*, New Series, 18, nos. 1-2, pp. 147-50.

52. Handa, Devendra 1969: Brief report of exploration by D.K. Handa at Sarangpur, *Indian Archaeology- A Review*, 1964-65, New Delhi, p. 33.

53. Heine-Geldern, R., 1936: 'Archaeological traces of the Vedic Aryans', *Journal of the Indian Society of Oriental Art*, IV, pp. 87-113.

54. Heine-Geldern, R., 1937: 'New Light on the Aryan migration to India', *Bulletin of the American Institute for Indian Art and Archaeology*, IV, pp. 7-16.

55. Heine-Geldern, R., 1956: 'The Coming of the Aryans and the End of the Harappan Civilization', *Man*, LVI, Art. No. 151, pp. 136-40.

56. Khan, F.A., 1958: 'Before Mohenjodaro: New Light on the Beginning of the Indus Valley Civilization from Recent Exacavation at Kot-Diji, *Illustrated London News*, May, 24, 1958, pp. 866-67.

57. Khan, F.A., 1965: 'Excavations at Kot-Diji', *Pakistan Archaeology*, No. 2, 1965.

58. Krishnaswami, V.D., 1953: 'Progress in Pre-History', *Ancient India*, No. 9, New Delhi, pp. 53-79.

59. Lal, B.B. (Brija Basi), 1951: 'Further Copper Hoards from the Gangetic Basin and a Review of the Problem', *Ancient India*, No. 7, pp. 20-39.

60. Lal, B.B., 1953: 'Protohistoric Investigations', *Ancient India*, No. 9, New Delhi, pp. 80-102.

61. Lal, B.B., 1954-55: 'Excavation at Hastinapura and other explorations in the Upper Ganga and Sutlej Basins 1950-52: New Light on the Dark Age between the end of the Harappa Culture and the Early

Historical Period', *Ancient India*, Nos. 10-11, pp. 10-11, 31-32.

62. Lal, B.B., 1961: Brief report of excavation at Kalibangan, district Ganganagar, *Indian Archaeology—A Review*, 1960-61, New Delhi, pp. 31-32.

63. Lal, B.B., 1962-63: 'A picture emerges–an assessment of the Carbon 14 datings of the protohistoric cultures of the Indo-Pakistan sub-continent', *Ancient India*, Nos. 18-19, pp. 208-221.

64. Lal, B.B., 1968: A Deluge ? Which Deluge ? Yet another fact of the Problem of the Copper Hoard Culture', *American Anthropologist*, Vol. 70, No.5, October, 1968, pp. 857-63.

65. Lal, B.B. (Brija Basi) and Thapar, B.K., 1962: Brief report of continued excavations at Kalibangan, district Ganganagar, *Indian Archaeology–A Review*, 1961-62, New Delhi, pp.39-44.

66. Lal, B.B. and Thapar, B.K., 1965: Brief report of continued excavations at Kalibangan, district Ganganagar, *Indian Archaeology- A Review*, 1962-63, New Delhi, pp. 20-31.

67. Lal, B.B. and Thapar, B.K., 1965-66: (under publication). Brief report of continued excavations at Kalibangan, district Ganganagar, *Indian Archaeology- A Review*, 1965-66, New Delhi.

68. Lal, B.B. and Thapar, B.K., 1967-1: Brief report of continued excavations at Kalibangan, district Ganganagar, *Indian Archaeology-A Review*, 1963-64, New Delhi, pp.30-37.

69. Lal, B.B. and Thapar, B.K., 1967-2: 'Excavations at Kalibangan: New Light on the Indus Civilization' *Cultural Forum*, Vol. IX, No. 4, July, 1967, pp. 78-88.

70. Lal, B.B. and Thapar B.K., 1968: Brief report of continued excavations at Kalibangan, district Ganganagar, *Indian Archaeology- A Review*, 1967-68, New Delhi, pp.42-45.

71. Lal, B.B. and Thapar B K., 1969: Brief report of continued excavations at Kalibangan, district Ganganagar, *Indian Archaeology-A Review*, 1964-65, New Delhi, pp. 35-39.

72. Lal (Dr.), B.B. (Bijen Behari), 1969: 'The Ochre-Coloured Pottery', *Potteries in Ancient India*, Patna, pp. 83-94.

73. Lohuizen de leeuw, J.E. Van, 1966: *De Protohistorische Culturen Van Voor-India en hun Datering*, Leiden.

74. Majumdar, N.G., 1934: *Explorations in Sind*, Memoirs of the Archaeological Survey of India, No. VIII, Delhi, 1934.

75. Mishra, V.D., 1965: Comments by V D. Mishra on R.C Gaur's paper on the 'Ochre-Coloured Pottery from Atranjikhera and its Significance', *Potteries in Ancient India*, Patna, p. 101.

76 Mishra, V.N., 1965: Comments by V.N. Mishra on A. Ghosh's paper on 'The Indus Civilization: Its Origins, Authors, Extent and Chronology', *Indian Prehistory: 1964*, Poona, pp. 147-48.

77. Piggot, Stuart, 1944: 'Prehistoric Copper Hoards in the Ganges Basin', *Antiquity*, XVIII, no. 72, pp. 173-82.

78. Piggot, Stuart, 1950: *Prehistoric India* (Penguin Books), Harmondsworth, p. 238.

79. Pruefer, Olaf, 1951: *Nalagarh 1951: Interim Report on the Excavations carried out at Dher Majra*, Calcutta, 1951.

80. Rao, S.R., 1969-1: 'The Harappan Ceramic Wares and the Devolution of the Harappa Culture', *Potteries in Ancient India*, Patna, pp. 257-60.

81. Rao, S.R., 1969-2: Comments by S.R. Rao on Krishna Deva's paper on the 'Problem of the Ochre-Coloured Pottery', *Potte'ies in Ancient India*, Patna, p.80.

82. Rishi, S.K., 1965: Notice of discovery by S.K. Rishi of Ochre-Coloured Ware at Jhinjhana, *Indian Archaeology- A Review*, 1962-63, New Delhi, p. 70.

83. Sankalia, H.D., 1961: Report of Copper Hoard from Khurdi, district Nagaur in Jodhpur Museum, *Indian Archaeology- A Review*, 1960-61, New Delhi, p. 66.

84. Sankalia, H.D., 1962: '*Prehistory and Protohistory in India and Pakistan*', Bombay, 1962, p. 223.

85. Sankalia, H.D., 1965-1: 'Traditional Indian Chronology and C- 14 dates of Excavated sites', *Indian Prehistory: 1964*, Poona, pp. 219-228.

86. Sankalia, H-D., 1965-2: Comments by H.D. Sankalia on A. Ghosh's paper on 'The Indus Civilization: Its Origins, Authors, Extent and Chronology', *Indian Prehistory: 1964*, Poona, p. 135.

87. Sharma, R.C., 1961: Notice of discovery by R.C. Sharma of Ochre-Coloured Ware at Manpur and Bhatpura, *Indian Archaeology- A Review*, 1960-61, New Delhi, p. 66.

88. Sharma, Y.D., 1954-1: Brief report of excavations at Rupar, *Indian Archaeology- A Review*, 1953-54, New Delhi, pp. 6-7.

89. Sharma, Y.D., 1954-2: Notice or reassessment of discoveries at Bikkun (Dher Majra), Bara, Kotli, Talapura, Chamkaur, and Hawara, *Indian Archaealogy-A Review*, 1953-54, New Delhi, p. 48.

90. Sharma, Y.D., 1955-1: Brief report of continued excavations at Rupar, *Indian Archaeology-A Review*, 1954-55, New Delhi, pp. 9-11.

91. Sharma, Y.D., 1955-2: Brief report of excavations at Bara, *Indian Archaeology- A Review*, 1954-55, New Delhi, pp. 9-10.

92. Sharma, Y.D , 1956: 'Past Patterns in living as unfolded by Excavations at Rupar', *Lalit Kala*, Nos. 1-2, 1955-56, pp. 121-29.

93. Sharma, Y.D., 1959: Brief report of excavations at Alamgirpur, district Meerut, *Indian Archaeology- A Review*, 1958-59, New Delhi, pp. 50-55.

94. Sharma, Y.D., 1961: 'Copper Hoards and Ochre Coloured Ware in Ganga Basin', *Summaries of Papers, Internation Conference on Asian Archaeology*, New Delhi.

95. Sharma, Y.D., 1964: 'Protohistoric Remains', *Archaeological Remains Monum.nts and Museums*, New Delhi, pp. 11-13.

96. Sharma, Y.D., 1965: Comments by Y.D. Sharma on A. Ghosh's paper on 'The Indus Civilization: Its Origins, Authors, Extent and Chronology', *Indian Prehistory: 1964*, Poona, pp. 131-35.

97. Shastri, H., 1915: 'Recent Additions to our knowledge of the Copper Age antiquities of the Indian Empire', *Journal of the Asiatic Society of Bengal*, New Series, XI, pp. 1-15.

98. Sinha, B.K., 1965-66: (under publication) Notice of discovery by B.K. Sinha of Ochre-Coloured Pottery near Kauria Ganj, district Aligarh, *Indian Archaeology- A Review*, 1965-66.

99. Sinha, B.P., 1969: 'Some Problems of Ancient Indian Potteries', *Potteries in Ancient India*, Patna, pp. 11-12.

100. Sinha, K.K., 1969: Comments by K.K. Sinha on Krishna Deva's paper on the 'problem of the Ochre-Coloured Pottery', *Potteries in Ancient India*, Patna, p.81.

101. Sinha, K.K., 1969: Comments by K.K. Sinha on R.C. Gaur's paper on the 'Ochre-Coloured Pottery from Atranjikhera and its Significance', *Potteries in Ancient India*, Patna, p. 100.

102. Smith, V.A.. 1905: 'The Copper Age and Prehistoric Bronze Implements of India, *Indian Antiquary*, XXXIV, pp. 229-44.

103. Soundara Rajan, K.V., 1965: Comments by K.V. Soundara Rajan on A. Ghosh's paper on 'The Indus Civilization: Its Origins, Authors, Extent and Chronology', *Indian Prehistory: 1964*, Poona, pp. 150-51.

104. Subba Rao, B., 1956: *The Personality of India*, Baroda, p. 43.

105. Suraj Bhan, 1964: 'The Late Phase of Harappa Culture' *Vishweshwaranand Indological Journal*, Vol. II, pt. II, September, 1964, pp. 344-52.

106. Suraj Bhan, 1967: 'New Light on the Ochre-Coloured Ware Culture', *Research Bulletin (Arts), Panjab University*, No. LVII (III), Chandigarh, 1967, pp.1-9.

107. Suraj Bhan, 1968: 'The Dawn of Civilization in Haryana', *Haryana Studies in History and Culture*, 1968, pp. 1-5.

108. Suraj Bhan, 1969: 'Excavations at Mitathal (Hissar) 1968', *Journal of Haryana Studies*, Vol. 4, No. 1, January 1969, pp. 1-15.

109. Suraj Bhan, 1970: Paper read at the annual conference of the Indian Archaeological Society, Nagpur, 1970.

110. Thapar, B.K., 1965: 'Relationship of the Indian Chalcolithic Cultures with West Asia', *Indian Prehistory: 1964*, Poona, pp 157-73, particularly p. 172.

111. Thapar B.K., 1970: 'Methodology in Archaeology', paper read at the annual conference of the Indian Archaeological Society, Nagpur, 1970.

112. Thapar, Romila, Dikshit, K N. and Sharma, R.P., 1969-70: (under publication) Brief report of excavation at Kaseri, district Meerut, by Romila Thapar and others, *Indian Archaeology-A Review*, 1969-70.

113. Tiwari, V.K., 1965-66: (under publication) Brief report of discovery by V.K. Tiwari of OCP at Aghiana, Sarurpur Taga, Shukhartal and Tauli, district Saharanpur, *Indian Archaeology-A Review*, 1965-66.

114. Wahal, LM. 1969-70: (under publication) Brief report of excavation by L.M. Wahal at Saipai Lichchwai, district Etawah, *Indian Archaeology- A Review*, 1969-70.

115. Wahal, L.M., 1969-70. (under publication) Brief report of discovery by L.M. Wahal of OCP at Nimsar, district Sitapur, *Indian Archaeology -A Review*, 1969-70

116. Vijay Kumar, 1969: Brief report of excavations by Vijay Kumar at Noh, district Bharatpur, *Indian Archaeology- A Review*, 1964-65, New Delhi, pp. 34-5.

117. Wheeler, Sir Mortimer, R.E., 1947: Harappa, 1946: the Defences and Cemetery R-37', *Ancient India*, No. 3, New Delhi.pp.58-30.

118. Wheeler, Sir Mortimer R.E., 1959: *Early India and Pakistan,* Bombay, pp. 118-27.

119. Wheeler, Sir Mortimer R.E., 1965: *Civilizations of the Indus Valley and beyond,* London, 1965, p. 98.

Supplementary Bibliography.

120. Gaur, R.C., 1966-67-1 (under publication) Brief report of discovery of OCP at Kharkhauda Kazimpur, district Meerut, *Indian Archaeology - A Review*, 1966-67.

121. Gaur, R.C., 1966-67-2 (under publication) Brief report of discovery of OCP at Lal-Qila, district Bulandshahr, *Indian Archaeology- A Review*, 1966-67.

122. Gaur, R.C. and S. Nurul Hasan, 1971: Brief report of excavations at Lal-Qila, district Bulandshahr, by R.C. Gaur and S. Nurul Hasan, *Indian Archaeology- A Review*, 1968-69, pp. 35-7.

123. Gaur R.C. and S.Nurul Hasan, 1969-70: (under publication) Brief report of continued excavations at Lal-Qila, district Bulandshahr, by R.C. Gaur and S.Nurul Hasan, *Indian Archaeology- A Review*, 1969-70.

124. Malik, S.C., 1968: *Indian Civilization : The Formative Period, Simla,* pp. 88-89.

125. Misra, V.D.and Misra, B.B., 1966-67: (under publication) Brief report of discovery of OCP in excavation at Baharia, district Shahjahanpur, *Indian Archaeology- A Review*, 1966-67.

126. Shankar Nath, 1966-67: (under publication) Brief report of discovery of OCP at Matki-Jharauli, Baundki, Ghanakhandi, Daudpur, Kabirpur, Lakhnauti Kalan, Chilehra, Asanwali, Piki, Sarkari Kumar, Bazidpur Majra, Sherpur (Gujar), Fatehpur (Gujar), Krishni, Reri Malakpur, Chhaparheri, Sarkari Shekh, Mohiuddinpur, Fatehpur (Jat), Chunehti, Gara, Pinjaura, Chhajpura, Kailaspur, Khatauli, Mandla, Salempur-Bhokri, *Indian Archaeology- A Review,* 1966-67.

127. Shankar Nath, 1967: Brief report of exploration by Shankar Nath at Bakarka, Budha-Khera, Ghathera and Hardakheri, district Saharanpur, *Indian Archaeology- A Review*, 1963-64, New Delhi,p.92.

128. Shankar Nath, 1968: Brief report of explorations by Shankar Nath at Alipura, Bahera-Khurd, Bhabri, Bhedeki (Mustahkam), Dhamola, Haribas, Kolkikalan, Kota, Mathana, Chunehti Shekh, Chouradeo, Nalhera-Bakal, Sobhri Khwaja, Abha, Dudh Bukhara (Mustahkam), Kalalhatti, Mahipura, Papreki, Pathori, Rasulpur, Rangel and Sabdalpur, district Saharanpur, *Indian Archaeology-A Review*, 1967-68, New Delhi, pp. 47-48.

129. Shankar Nath, 1971: Brief report of exploration by Shankar Nath at Mirpur and Faridpur-urf-Mandowal, district Saharanpur, *Indian Archaeology- A Review*, 1968-69, p. 41.

130. Shankar Nath, 1969: Brief report of exploration by Shankar Nath at Kajipura, Nirpalpur, Rajdhana and Sikri, district Saharanpur, *Indian Archaeology- A Review*, 1964-65, New Delhi, p. 43.

131. Shankar Nath, 1969-70: (under publication) Brief report of discovery by Shankar Nath of OCP at Anwarpur Baroli, district Saharanpur, *Indian Archaeology- A Review*, 1969-70.

132. Sharma, R.P., 1971: Brief report of discovery by R.P. Sharma of OCP at Malehra and Nahli, district Meerut, *Indian Archaeology- A Review*, 1968-69, p. 40.

APPENDIX I

BIBLIOGRAPHY OF THE NBP WARE

(This bibliography has been compiled by Shri Ramesh Chandra Agrawal, Shri Shanker Nath and the Editor. It includes reports on main excavated sites, which have yielded the NBP Ware. The 'Indian Archaeology—A Review' contains many notices of the discovery of the NBP Ware in surface exploration. All such notices have been brought under the title 'Indian Archaeology—A Review', at the end indicating the year to which the publication relates, and not the year in which it has been actually published. Ed.)

1. Altekar, A.S., 1951: *Report on Kumrahar Excavations*, Patna.

2. Ansari, Z.D., 1961: 'Evolution of Pottery Forms and Fabrics' *Marg*, Vol. XIV, No. 3, Bombay, p. 8.

3. Bhardwaj, H.C., 1969: 'Some Technical Observations on NBP Ware Slip', *Potteries in Ancient India*, Patna, pp. 188-92.

4. Deshpande, M.N., 1971: 'Archaeological Sources for the Reconstruction of the History of Sciences of India', *Indian Journal of History of Sciences*, No. 1, Vol. 6, p. 19.

5. Deva, Krishna, and Mishra, Vijayakanta 1961: *Vaishali Excavations: 1950*, Vaishali.

6. Deva, Krishna and Wheeler, Sir Mortimer R.E., 1946: 'Northern Black Polished Ware', Appendix A to No. 14 below, *Ancient India*, No. 1, 1946, pp. 55-56.

7 Dikshit M.G., 1952: *Tripuri*, Bhopal.

8. Gadre, M.B., 1940: 'Sanchi', *Annual Administration Report of the Archaeological Department, Gwalior State, 1938-39*, Gwalior.

9. Gaur, R.C. and Hasan Nurul S., 1964: *Excavations at Atranjikhera* (A preliminary Report), Aligarh, (Cyclostyled copy).

10. Gaur, R.C., 1969: 'A Note on the NBP Ware,' *Potteries in Ancient India*, Patna.

11. Ghosh, A., 1947-48: 'Taxila (Sirkap), 1944-45,' *Ancient India*, No. 4, New Delhi, pp. 41-84.

12. Ghosh A., 1950: 'The Historical Period', *Archaeology in India*, New Delhi, 1950.

13. Ghosh, A., 1951: 'Rajgir, 1950', *Ancient India*, No. 7 New Delhi, 1951, pp. 66-78.

14. Ghosh, A. and Panigrahi, K.C., 1946: 'Pottery of Ahichchhatra (U.P.)' *Ancient India*, No. 1, January, 1946, pp. 37-59.

15. Goswami, K.G., 1948: *Excavations at Bangarh*, Calcutta, p. 27.

16. Hegde, K.T.M., 1962: 'Technical Studies in NBP Ware,' *Journal of the M.S. University of Baroda*, Vol. XI, No. 1.

17. Hedge, K.T.M., 1966: *Current Science*, Vol. 35, Bangalore, 1966.

18. Hedge, K.T.M. 1970: 'Physics and Chemistry in Indian Archaeology', paper read at the annual conference of the Indian Archaeological Society, Nagpur, 1970.

19. Lal, B.B. (Brija Basi), 1948: 'Sisupalgarh, 1948: An Early Historical Fort in Eastern India,' *Ancient India*, No. 5, New Delhi, p. 79.

20. Lal, B.B., 1954-55: 'Excavation at Hastinapura and other explorations in the Upper Ganga and Sutlej Basins, 1950-52', *Ancient India*, Nos. 10-11, New Delhi, pp. 5-151, particularly pp. 50-52, 143-46.

21. Lal (Dr.), B.B. (Bijen Behari), 1956: 'Archaeological Chemistry, D-Research', *Indian Archaeology-A Review*, 1955-56, New Delhi, pp. 56-57.

22. Lal (Dr.), B.B. 1960: 'Archaeological Chemistry, Analysis and Research', *Indian Archaeology—A Review, 1959-60*, pp. 120-21.

23. Marshal, Sir John. H., 1904-05: 'Excavations at Sarnath,' *Annual Report of the Archaeological Survey of India*. 1904-1905, Calcutta, 1908, pp. 59. ff. (Account of excavations continues in the Reports for 1906-7, 1907-08, 1914-15, 1919-20, 1921-22, 1927-28).

24. Marshall, Sir John H., 1909-10: 'Excavations at Bhita', *Annual Report of the Archaeological Survey of India*, Calcutta, pp. 40 ff.

25. Marshall, Sir John H., 1913-14: 'Evcavations at Basarh', *Annual Report of the Archaeological Survey of India, Calcutta*, pp. 98 ff

26. Marshall, Sir John H., 1940: *Monuments of Sanchi*, 3 Vols., Delhi.

27. Misra, V D., 1969: 'Pottery of Kausambi,' *Potteries in Ancient India*, Patna, 1969, pp. 207-08.

28. Narain, Lala Aditya, 1966: 'Associated Antiquities of the NBP Ware with special reference to Bihar,' *Potteries in Ancient India*, Patna, pp. 163-202.

29. Nigam, J.S., 1961: 'Northern Black Polished Ware', *Marg*, No. 3, Vol. XIV, Bombay.

30. Ramachandran, T.N., 1951: 'Tamralipti (Tamluk)' *Artibus Asiae*, Vol XIV, 3.

31. Rawson, P.S. 1943: 'The Surface Treatment of Early Indian Pottery', *Man*, 1953, Art. No. 58, pp. 41-42.

32. Roy, Sita Ram 1963: 'Northern Black Polished Ware in Bihar,' *Potteries in Ancient India*, Patna, 1969, pp. 167-73

33. Sahay, Sachchidanand, 1969: 'Origin and spread of the Northern Black Polished Ware', *Potteries in Ancient India*, Patna, 1969, pp. 146-54.

34. Sahni, D.R., 1936: *Excavations at Bairat*, Jaipur.

35. Sana Ullah Khan 1946: Report reproduced in No. 14 above, *Ancient India*, No. 1, January, 1946, p. 58.

36. Sankalia, H.D., 1951: 'Ancient and prehistoric Maharashtra', *Journal of Bombay Branch of the Royal Asiatic Society*, XXVII.

37. Sankalia, H.D., 1955: *Report on Excavations at Nasik and Jorwe, 1950-51*, Poona.

38. Sankalia, H.D., 1958: *The excavations at Maheshwar and Navdatoli, 1952-53*, Poona.

39. Sankalia, H.D., 1960: *From History to Prehistory at Nevasa, 1954-56*, Poona.

40. Sankalia, H.D., and Dikshit, M.G., 1952: *Excavations at Brahmpuri (Kolhapur), 1945-46*, Poona.

41. Sharma, G.R., 1960: *Excavations at Kaushambi*, Allahabad, 1960.

42. Sharma, G.R., 1969: *Excavations at Kaushambi, 1949-50*, Memoirs of the Archaeological Survey of India, No. 74, New Delhi.

44. Sharma, Y.D., 1953: 'Exploration of Historical Sites', *Ancient India*, No. 9, New Delhi, pp. 116-69.

45. Sharma, Y.D., 1955-56: 'Past Patterns in living as unfolded by Exacavations at Rupar', *Lalit Kala*, Nos. 1-2, New Delhi, pp. 121-29.

46. Sharma, Y.D., 1964: 'Remains of Early Historical Cities,' *Archaeological Remains Monuments and Museums*, Part I, New Delhi, pp. 43-84.

47. Sinha, K.K., 1967: *Excavations at Sravasti : 1959*, Varanasi.

48. Sinha, K.K., 1969: 'The N.B.P. Ware—Fresh Hypothesis in the light of Sravasti Evidence,' *Potteries in Ancient India*, Patna, pp. 174-84.

49. Thapar, B.K., 1964-65: 'Prakash: 1955,—A Chalcolithic Site in Tapti Valley, *Ancient India*, Nos. 20-21, New Delhi, pp. 13, 71-5.

50. Wheeler Sir Mortimer R.E., 1959: *Early India and Pakistan*, London, 1959, pp. 26-33.

Indian Archaeology—A Review

1953-54: Rupar, pp. 6-7; Maheshwar, district Nimar, p. 8; Rajgir, district Patna, p. 9; Kausambi, district Allahabad, p. 9; Kumrahar, Patna, p. 9; Amaravati, district Guntur, p. 38.

1954-55: Purana-Qila, Delhi, p. 19; Mathura, p. 15; Rajgir, district Patna, p. 16; Hathras, district Aligarh, p. 61; Baligarh, district Darbhanga, p. 61; Dharhara, district Purnea, p. 61.

1955-56: Nagda, district Ujjain, p. 14; Ujjain, p. 19; Kannauj, district Farukhabad, p. 19; Kausambi, district Allahabad, p. 20; Pataliputra (Patna), p. 22; Poiya, Renuka, Mahuar, district Agra, p. 70; Noh, Bhej, district Bharatpur, p. 71; Aring, Sanketban, district Mathura, p. 71; Sankisa, district Farukhabad, p. 71; Lakshman-Tila, Lucknow, p. 71; Erachh, Chhota Belna, district Jhansi, p. 71; Mats Kisanpur, Bara, Bithur, district Kanpur, p. 71; Ayodhya, district Faizabad, p. 71; Sravasti, district Gonda-Bahraich, p. 71; Singraur, district Allahabad, p. 71; Lakneswar Dih, district Ballia, p. 71; Bodh-Gaya, district Gaya, p. 71; Pirnagra Deorhi, district Monghyr, p. 71; Sonitpur, district Gaya, p. 71; Chandraketur-garh (Berachampa), district 24- Parganas, p. 71.

1956-57: Prabhas Patan, district Sorath, p. 17; Sonepur, district Gaya, p. 19; Ujjain, p. 24; Kausambi, district Allahabad, p. 29; Jajmau, district Kanpur, p. 29; Lakhneswar-dih, district Ballia, p. 29; Chandraketugarh (Berachampa), district 24-Parganas, pp. 30 and 81.

1957-58: Vaisali, district Muzaffarpur, p. 11; Ter, district Osmanabad, p. 23; Navda Toli, district Nimar, p. 32; Kausambi, district Allahabad, pp. 47-8; Jajmau, district Kanpur, p. 49; Rajghat, district Varanasi, p. 50; Chandraketugarh, district 24-Parganas, p. 51; Lahar, district Bhind, p. 67; Tewar, district Jabalpur, p. 68; Awara, district Mandsor, p. 68; Daulatabad or Husainabad, district Bijnor, p. 69; Bahua, district Fatehgarh, p. 69; Ujhan, Umaragarh, district Kanpur, p. 69.

1958-59: Amaravati, district Guntur, p. 5; Vaisali, district Muzaffarpur, p. 12; Barata, district Bhind, p. 26; Chosla, district Ajmer, p. 45; Gondi, district Jaipur, p. 45; Kausambi, district Allahabad, pp. 46-47; Sravasti (Mahet), district Bahraich, pp. 47-50; Nathnagar, district Bhagalpur, p. 68; Chirand, district Saran, p. 68; Sauripur, district Agra, p. 74; Mahnydih, district Allahabad, p. 74; Bindual, Moraon, Tickar, Kilarman, district Fatehpur, p. 75; Baigar, district Varanasi, p. 75.

1959-60: Sonpur, district Gaya, p. 14; Vaisali, district Muzaffarpur, p. 16; Broach, p. 19; Awra, district Mandasor, p. 24; Chandraketugarh, district 24-Parganas, p. 51; Asohua, Barauli, Jamdara, Mow, district Bhind, p. 69; Pipargaon, Bhargain, district Etah, p. 75; Toharganj, Masaondih, Devachandpur, district Ghazipur, p. 75.

1950-61: Chebrolu, district Guntur, p. 1; Sonpur, district Gaya, p. 5; Vaisali, district Muzaffarpur, p. 6; Eran, district Sagar, p. 18; Sankara, district Aligarh, p. 33; Draupadighat (Allahabad), Chilla, Govindpur, Salori, Dariabad, Mirpur, district Allahabad, p. 33; Kausambi, district Allahabad, p. 34; Atranjikhera, district Etah, p. 35; Rajghat (Varanasi), p. 37; Chandraketugarh, district 24- Parganas, p. 39; Burhanpur, district Nimar, p. 60; Gumad, Akbarpur-Baroth, district Rohtak, p. 65; Takhawan, Gone-Umargarh, Nokhera, district Etah, p. 66; Khaga, district Fatehpur, p. 67; Dadupur, Qila Muhammadi Nagar, district Lucknow, p. 67; Kodar, district Mainpuri, p. 67; Kashipur, district Nainital, p. 67.

1961-62: Karangarh, district Bhagalpur, p. 3; Sonpur, district Gaya, pp. 4-5; Khakharadih, Sarahiyadih, district Monghyr, p. 5; Vaisali, district Muzaffarpur, pp. 5-7; Rajgir, district Patna, p. 7; Chirand, Mohamadagarh, Manjhigarh, Muiyagarh, Sitalpur, district Saran, p. 9; Nagal, district Broach, pp. 11-12; Kaundanpur, district Amraoti, p. 29;

Ahar, district Udaipur, p. 45; Kausambi, district Allahabad, p. 51; Jhusi, Lachhagir, Sathar, Jalalpur, Sringraur, district Allahabad, p. 52; Bara-Achhola, district Allahabad, pp. 52-53; Bankatha, district Azamgarh, p. 53; Bhitari, district Ghazipur, p. 53; Tikari, district Varanasi, p. 53; Ayodhya, district Faizabad, p. 53; Prahaladpur, Saunakdih, district Varanasi, p. 53; Chandravati, Kailasa, Bairat, district Varanasi, p. 54; Oraghar, district Gonda, p. 56; Faridinagar, Mandiaon, district Lucknow, p. 56; Sohagaura, district Gorakhpur, p. 56; Jajmau, Barhat, district Kanpur, p. 57; Aong, Bhanwant, Ilahabas, Kaurara-Buzurg, Mandai, Parham, Pharengi, Salempur, Perhina, Shamsher-ganj-Maholi, Sirsaganj, Uncha-Islamabad, district Mainpuri, p. 57; Thana, district Unnao, p. 57; Rajghat (Varanasi), p. 58; Chandraketugarh, district 24- Parganas, p. 62; Tilaurakot, district Taulihawa (Nepal), pp. 73-74; Akoda, district Bhind, p. 98; Atranjikhera, district Etah, p. 103.

1962-63: Balirajgarh, district Darbhanga, p. 5; Rajgir, district Patna, p. 5; Chirand, district Saran, p. 6; Bairat, district Jaipur, p. 31; Kausambi, district Allahabad, p. 33; Deoriya, Pipari, district Basti, p. 33; Marchayadih, Papaurdih, district Deoria, p. 33; Bajre-Tiket, Mahal, Zafarabad, district Jaunpur, p. 33; Barkad, Bhavan Jharia, Kamhari, Kusaha-Kusi, Mahauwan, Rudauli, Saranyya, Sultanpur, Upadhi, Ronp, district Mirzapur, p. 34; Banda, Sikandarpur, Takiyapur, Bairat, Itwan, Janso-ki-Marai, Magaraur, Prahaladpur, Leelapur, Sirpat-Baram, district Varanasi, p. 34; Atranjikhera, district Etah, p. 34; Shampur, district Hardoi, p. 36; Dabka, Godhe, Parichhatgarh, Shondat, district Meerut, pp. 36-7; Bhuma, Jatwara, Kailapur,, Kaithora, Khai-Khera, Kheri-Sarai, Sikrera, district Muzaffarnagar, p. 37; Manwa, Nazirabad, district Sitapur, p. 39; Bethar, Dariyapur, Deeh Kahinjar, Newal, Pariar, district Unnao, p. 39; Prahaladpur, district Varanasi, p. 41; Rajghat, district Varanasi, p. 41; Chandraketugarh, district 24-Parganas, pp. 46-47; Khera, district Aligarh, p. 70; Saton, district, Fatehpur, p. 70; Bairi, Sanon, district Kanpur, p. 70; Lakshman-tila, Lucknow, p. 70; Kotasur, district Birbhum, p. 71.

1963-64: Dharanikota, district Guntur, p. 2; Chirand, district Saran, p. 8; Buxur (Charittarvan), district Shahabad, p. 8; Nagara, district Kaira, p. 10; Eran, district Sagar, p. 16; Besnagar, district Vidisha, p. 16; Kardhan, Mirzapur, Suga (Amadalpur), Tandwal, Kakrauni, Sugh, district Ambala, pp. 27-28; Noh, district Bharatpur, p. 28; Kausambi, district Allahabad, p. 40; Ajaneraghar, Bhimapur - Dih, Bijalipur, Gadabirghar, Masumpur, district Ballia, p. 43; Chauthi-ka-kot, Orarheen-ka-kot, Sidat- ka-kot, Wazidpur-ka-kot, district Ghazipur, p. 43; Dih, Dih-Darari, Kota, Kota-ki-Mari, Kotabarahi, Mehada ka-kot, Rohniya-ka-kot, district Jaunpur, p. 43, Benh-ki-kot, Dhuri-Kusi-Dih, Illia, Latifshah

Dam, district Varanasi, p. 43; Ahichchhatra, district Bareilly, pp. 43-44; Abbasganj, Bahukasiktar,Bakarganj, Bharvalia Babu, Kopia, Udsara, district Basti, p. 45; Araon-Jagdish, Barhayapur, Bharvalia, Jadappatti, Dumhara, Dhuriyapur, Jauharabad, Jhauan, Madaraha, Mau-Buzurg, Pakari-Dubey, Sikariganj, Trilokapur, Uruva, district Gorakhpur, p. 45; Atranjikhera, district Etah, p. 49; Bhaintari, district Moradabad, p 53; Sambhal, district Moradabad, p. 92. Nurnagar, district Muzaffarnagar, pp. 53-54; Rajghat, district Varanasi, pp. 58-59; Chandraketugarh (Khana-Mihirer-Dhipi and Itakhola), district 24- Pargans, pp. 63-64; Gadka-Chak, district Bhagalpur; p. 86; Bhadauni, district Gaya, p. 86; Bhadras, district Kanpur, p. 91.

1964-65: Chirand, district Saran, p. 7; Ujjain, p. 18; Kayatha, district Ujjain, pp. 13-19; Besnagar, district Vidisha, pp. 19-20; Autha, district Gurgaon, pp. 33-34; Noh, district Bharatpur, pp. 34-35; Ahichchhatra, district Bareilly, p. 39; Bhitari, Jauharganj, Kot, Rangmahal, Masaon, district Ghazipur, p. 42; Budhakhera, Lodhipur, Mandowala, Raipur, district Saharanpur, pp. 43 - 44; Rajghat, district, Varanasi, p. 44; Pandu-Rajar-Dhibi, district Burdwan, p. 48; Bhadsa, district Kanpur, p. 76; Pirthinagar, Nazirpur, district Lucknow, p. 76; Pakara-Buzurg, Panhan, disirict Unnao, p. 76.

1965-66: (under publication) Oriup, district Bhagalpur, Maner, district Patna; Buxar, district Shahabad (Arrah), Tripuri, district Jabalpur; Paithan, district Aurangabad; Sugh, district Ambala; Poiya, Vaman, district Agra; Amanullahpur alias Mahrana, district Bulandshahr; Atranjikhera, district Etah; Bhishmapur (Farrukhabad), Kampil, district Farrukhabad; Shahabad, Lakhmapur, district Hardoi; Bithur, district Kanpur; Gaddi-ka-Than, Garcha-Gopalapur, district Jaunpur; Masaon, district Ghazipur; Attawa, Jhangirabad, Lalpur, district Kanpur; Mandoni, Bina, Hulaskhera, district Lucknow; Rajghat, district Varanasi; Chandraketugarh, district 24-Parganas, Maharajganj, district Saran; Kakrahta, district Jabalpur; Galatha, district Fatehpur; Shahabad, district Hardoi.

1966-67 (under publication): Oriup, district Bhagalpur; Tripuri, district Jabalpur; Noh, district Bharatpur; Jalalabad, Nigohi, district Shahjahanpur; Kausambi, district Allahabad; Ghosi, district Azamgarh; Mahal, Naipore, Mahadeo-ka-kila, district Jaunpur; Sonkh, district Mathura; Kalayat, district Jind.

1967-68: Manjhi, district Saran, p 9; Kayatha, district Ujjain, p. 25; Behhar Jungle, district Basti, p. 45; Atranjikhera, district Etah, p. 45; Galath, district Fatehpur, p. 46; Bihupur, Padri Lalpur, Jahagirabad, district Kanpur, p. 46; Masaon, district Ghazipur, pp. 46-47; Karchalipur, Musanagar, district Kanpur, p. 47; Bauthra, Kalli

Najhagaman Pachchim, Tikri, district Lucknow, p. 47; Sarai Mohana, district Varanasi, p. 49.

1968-69: Champa, Jahangira, district Bhagalpur, p. 4; Chirand, district Saran pp. 5-6; Noh, district Bharatpur, p. 26; Ghosei, district Azamgarh, pp. 35. Chauharjan, Nevari, district Pratapgarh, p. 35; Ghajanpur, district Sultanpur, p. 35; Atranjikhera, district Etah, pp. 37-8; Chandanpur, Reona, Karchalipur, Jajmau, district Kanpur p. 39; several sites. district Sitapur, p. 39; Ahmadpur Khaira, Umed Khera, Utrawan, district Lucknow, p. 40; Amini, district Fatehpur, p. 70.

1969-70: (under publication) Champa, district Bhagalpur; Purana-Qila (Delhi); Jharda, Narayangad, district Mandasor; Sanghol, district Ludhiana; Diha, district Allahabad; Etawah Fort (Etawah), Chakannagarkhada, district Etawah; Ayodhya, district Faizabad; Kurain, district Kanpur; Barailia, district Lucknow; Nimsor, Manwan, district Sitapur; Madanpur, district Deoria; Bahri, district Jaunpur.

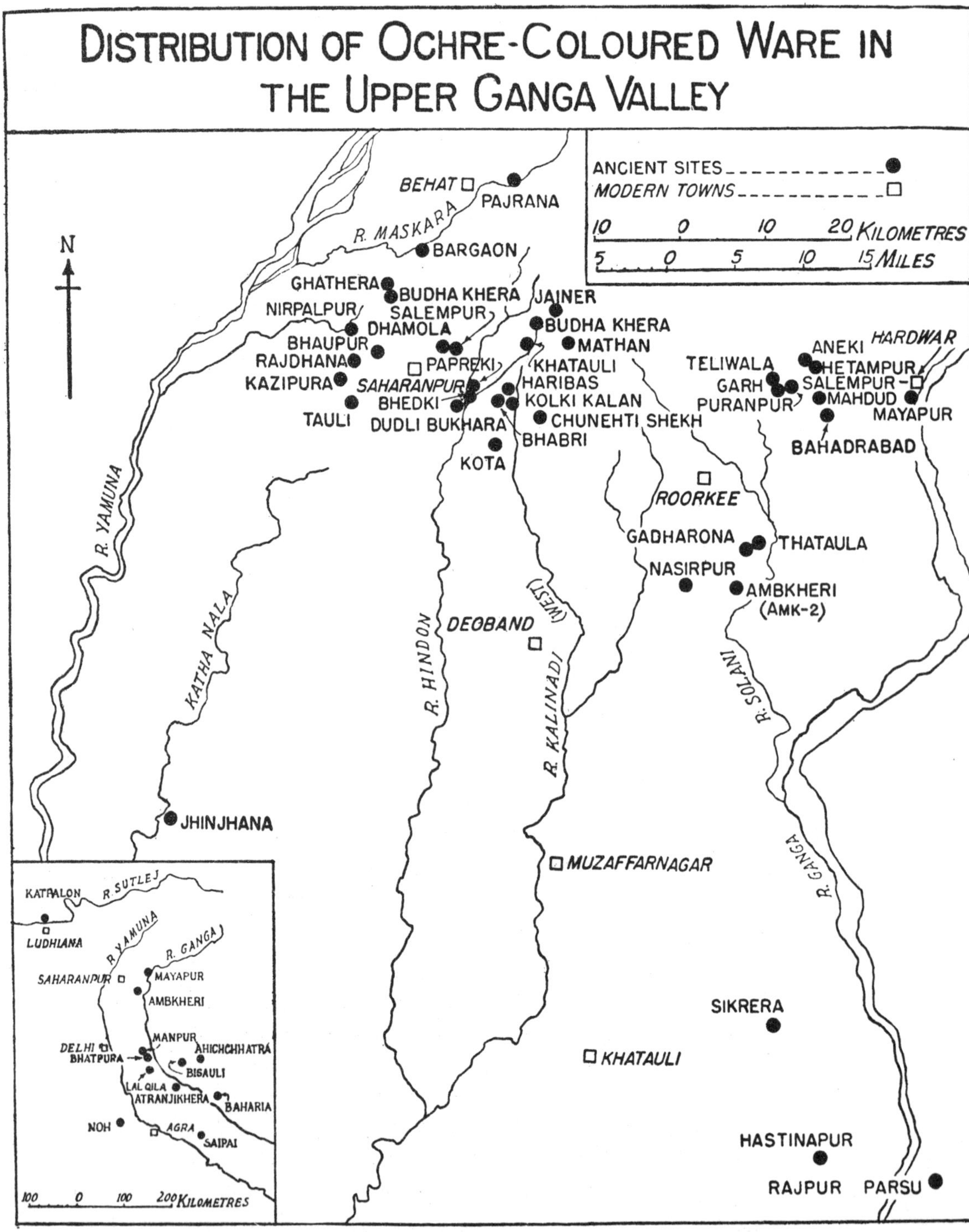

Fig. 1 Distribution map of OCP in the upper Ganga valley.

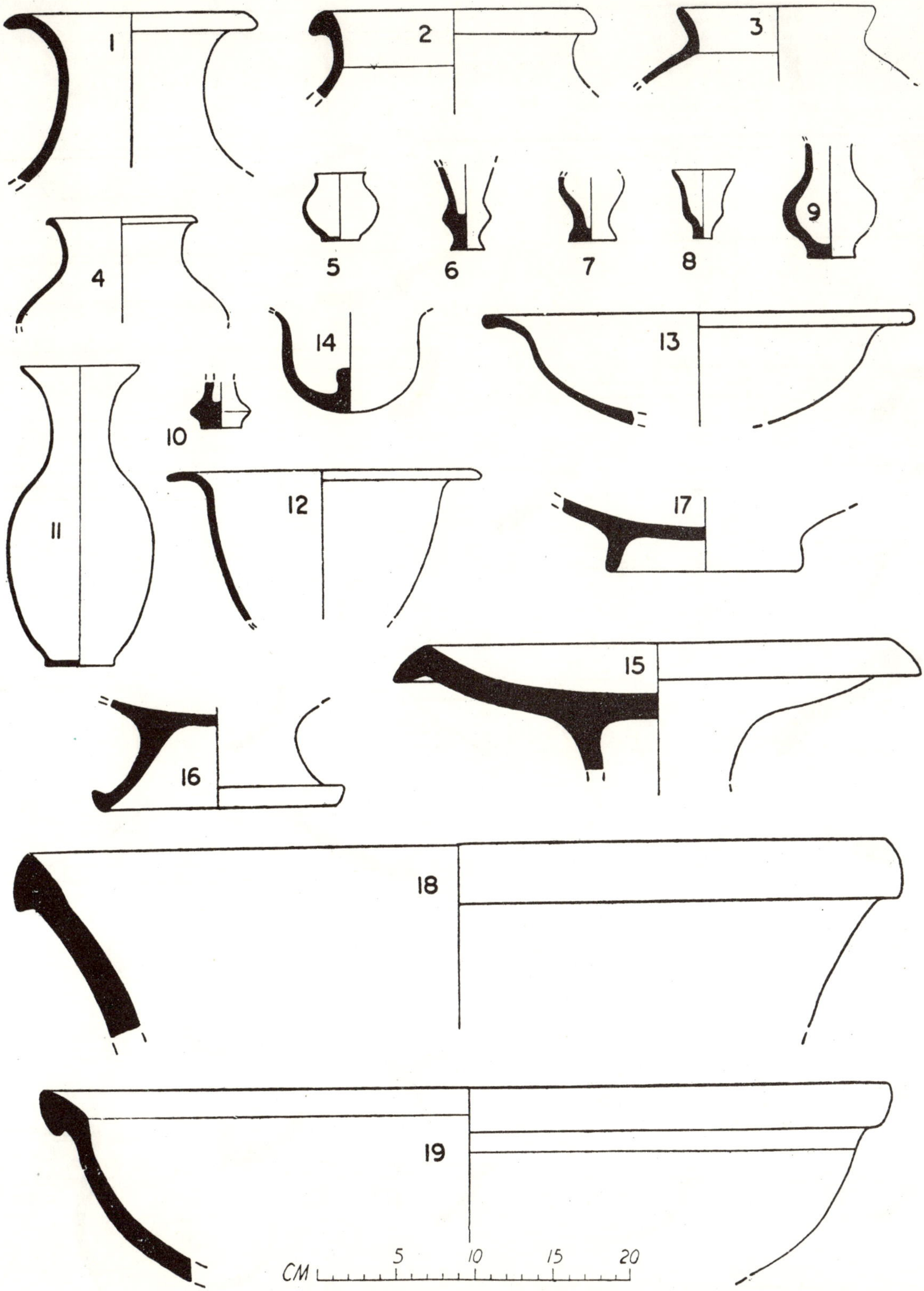

Fig. 2 Pottery shapes from Ambkheri

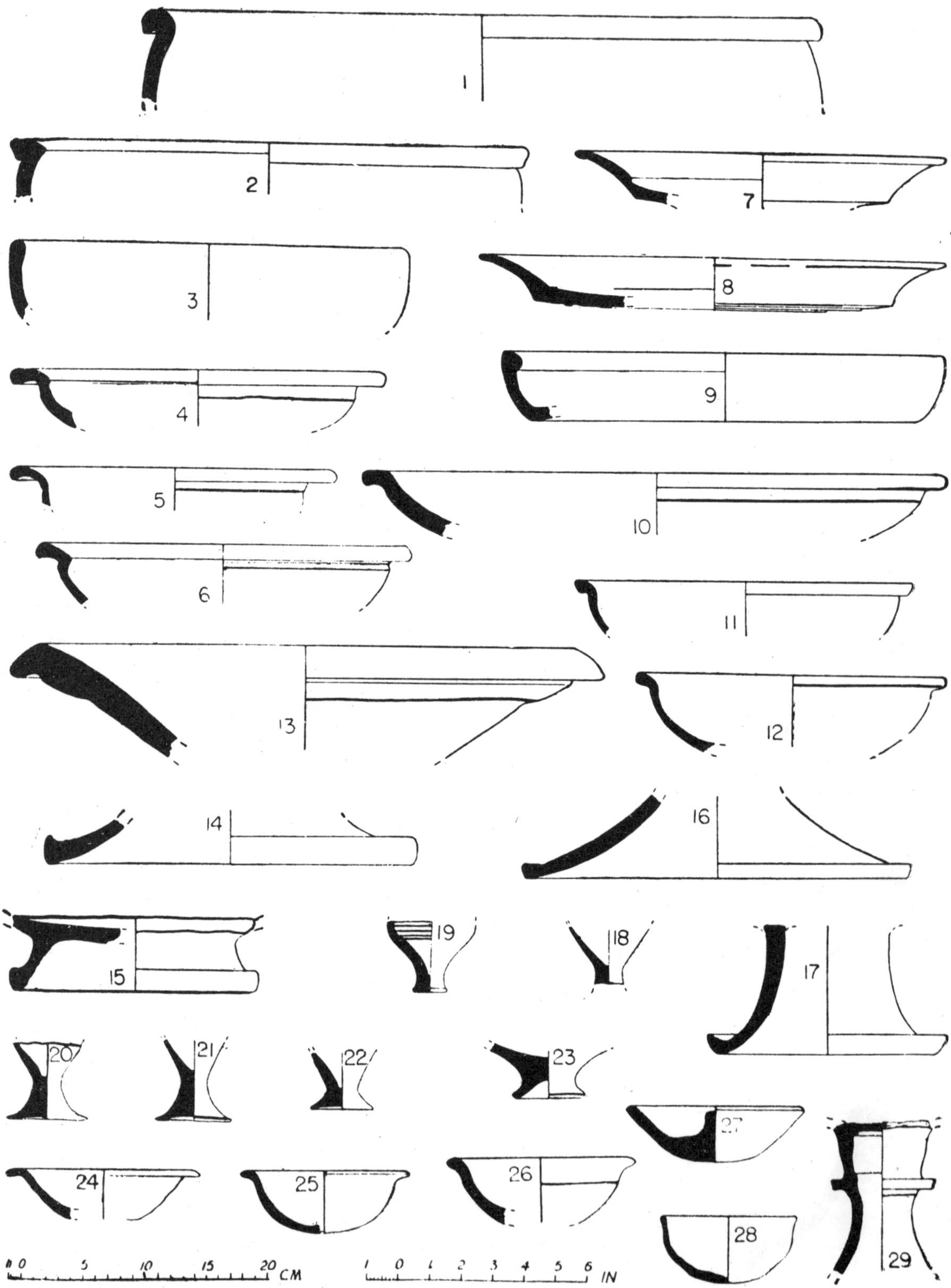

Fig. 3 Pottery shapes from Bargaon

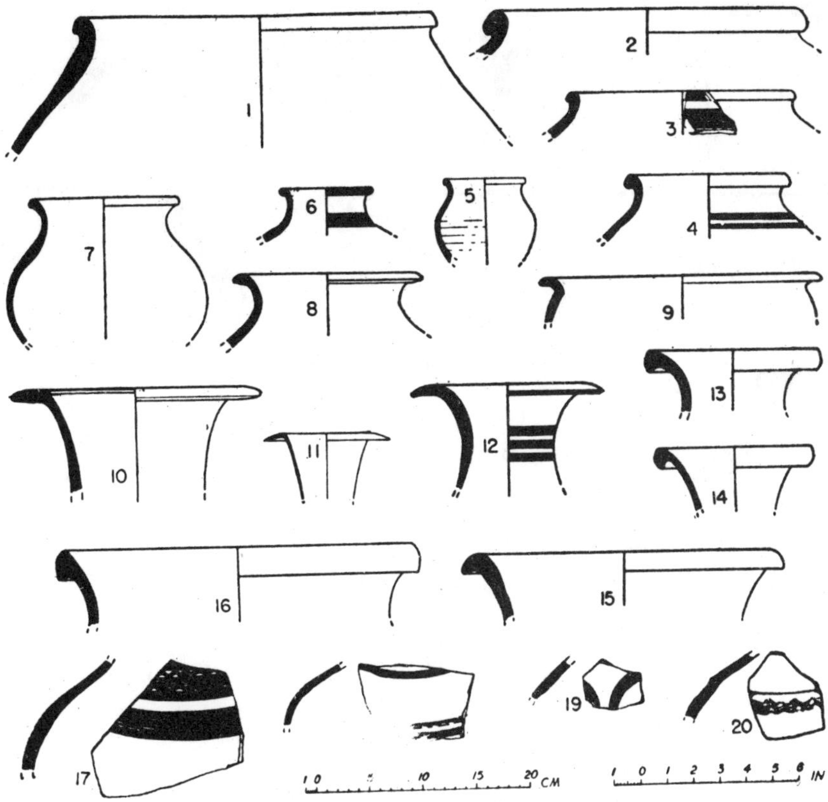

Fig. 4 Pottery shapes from Bargaon

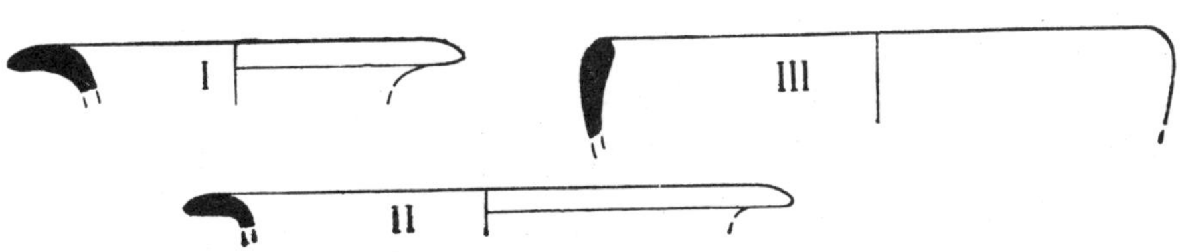

Fig. 5 OCP shapes from Hastinapura

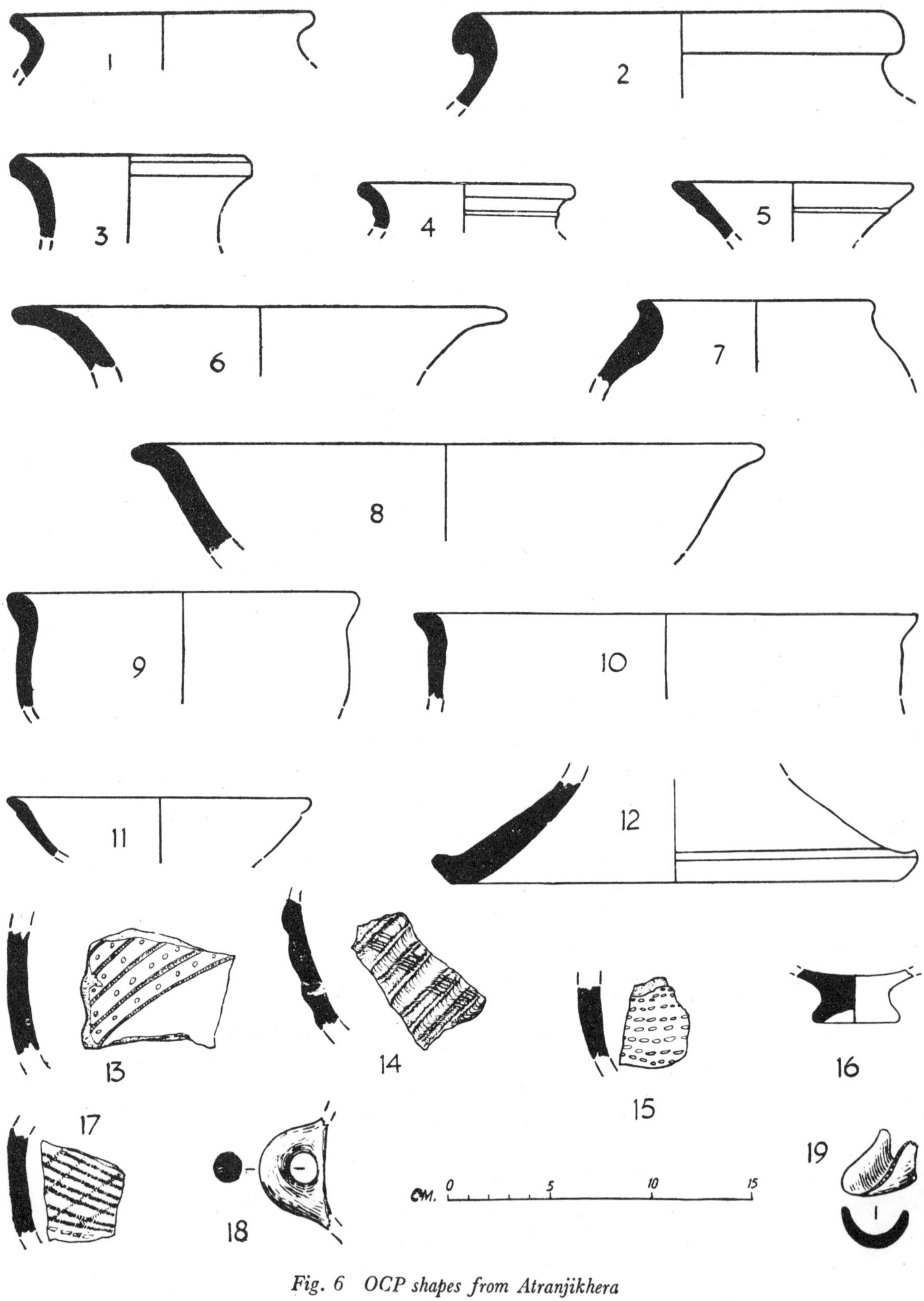

Fig. 6 OCP shapes from Atranjikhera

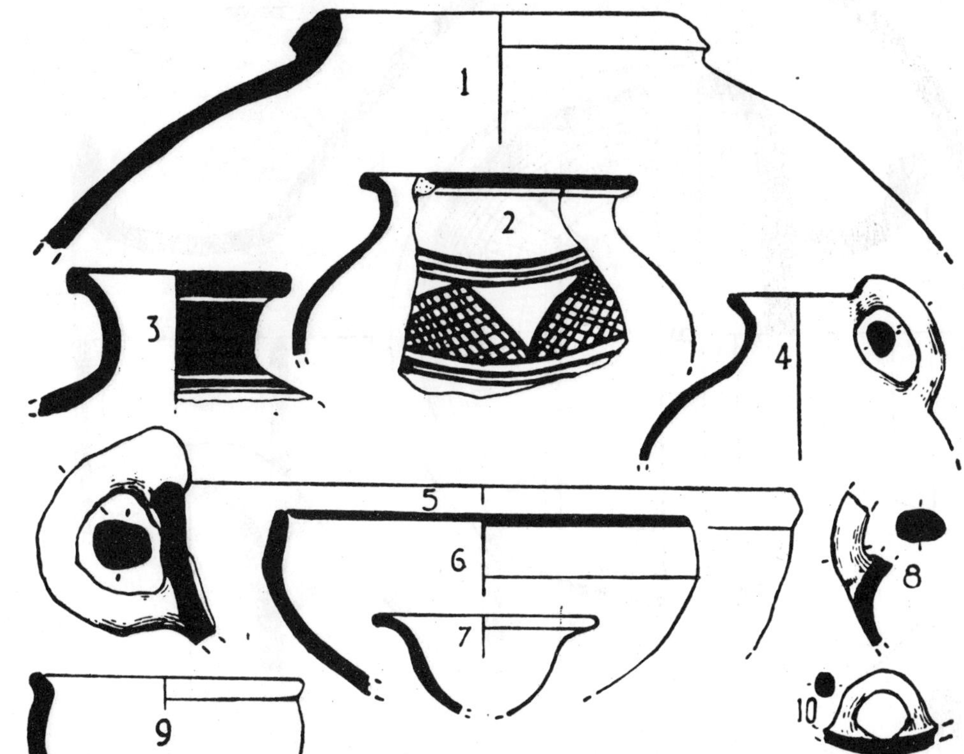

Fig. 7 Pottery shapes from Lal-Qila.

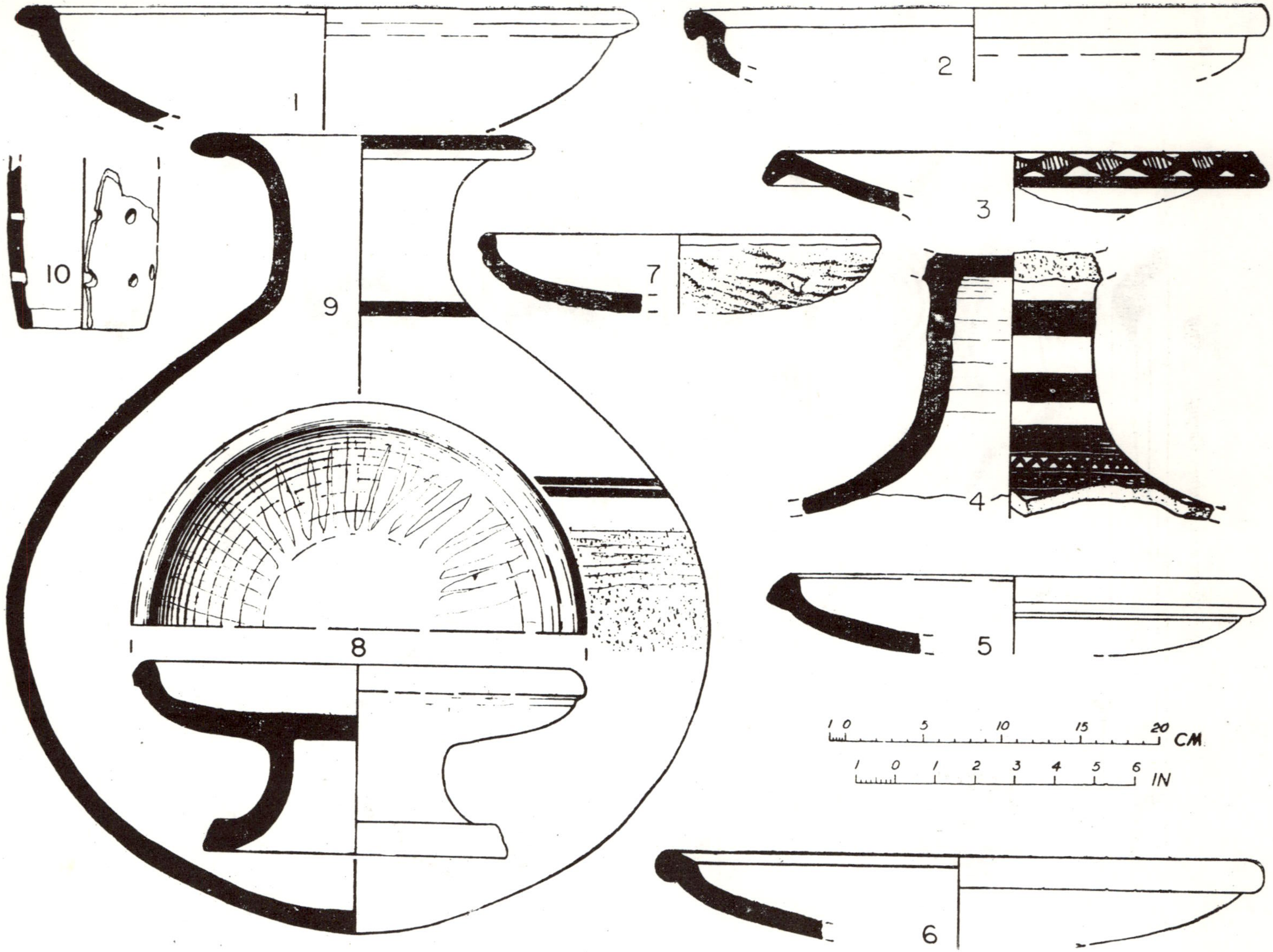

Fig. 8 Pottery shapes from Bara

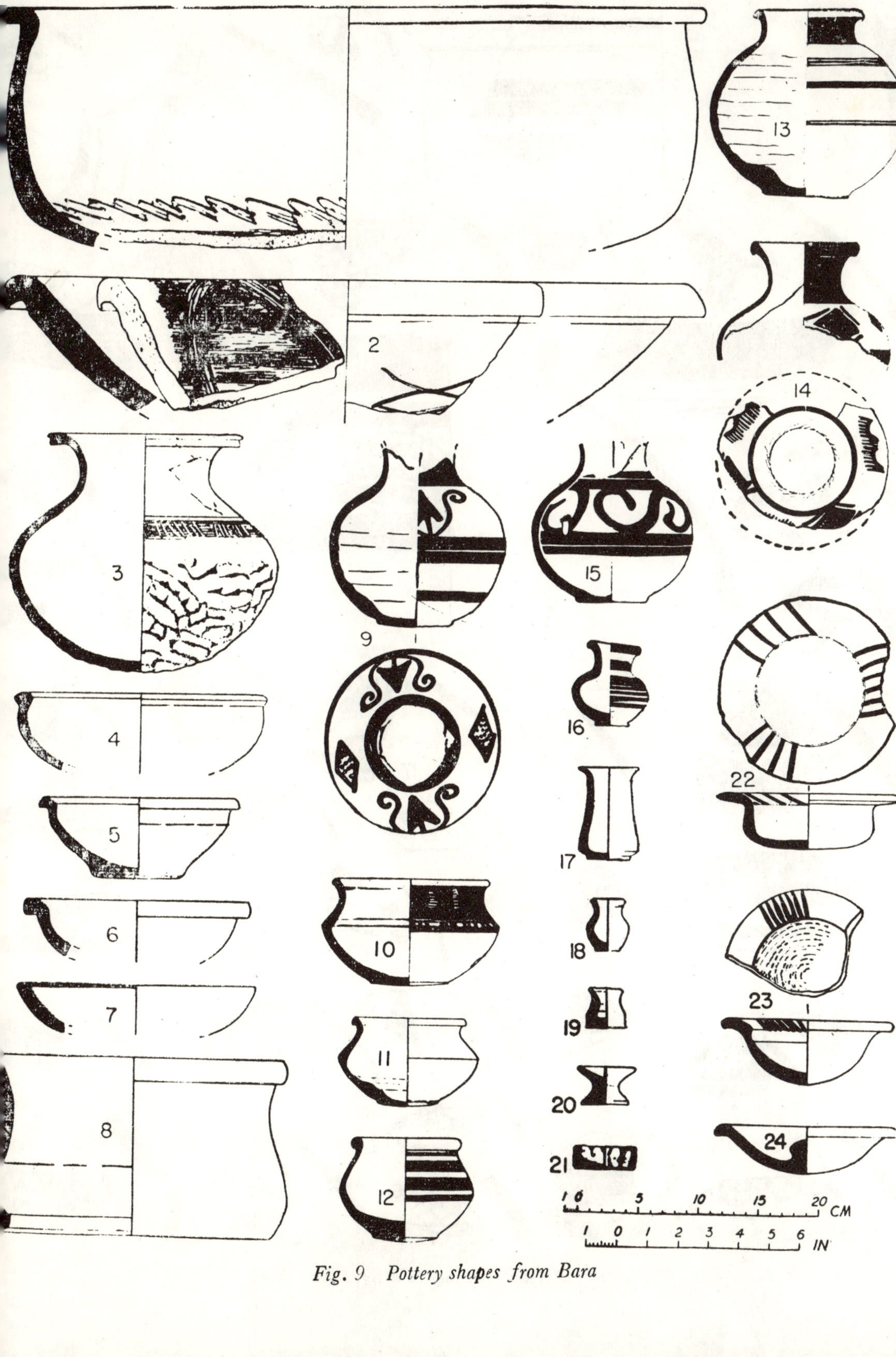

Fig. 9 Pottery shapes from Bara

Fig. 10 Painted and incised designs from Bara

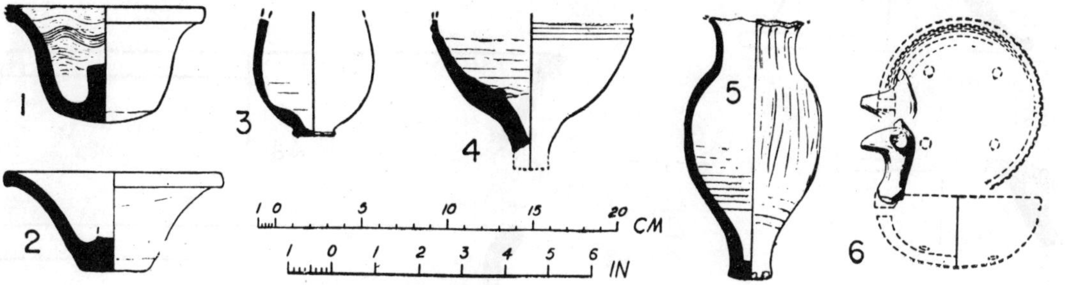

Fig. 11 Harappan pottery from Bara

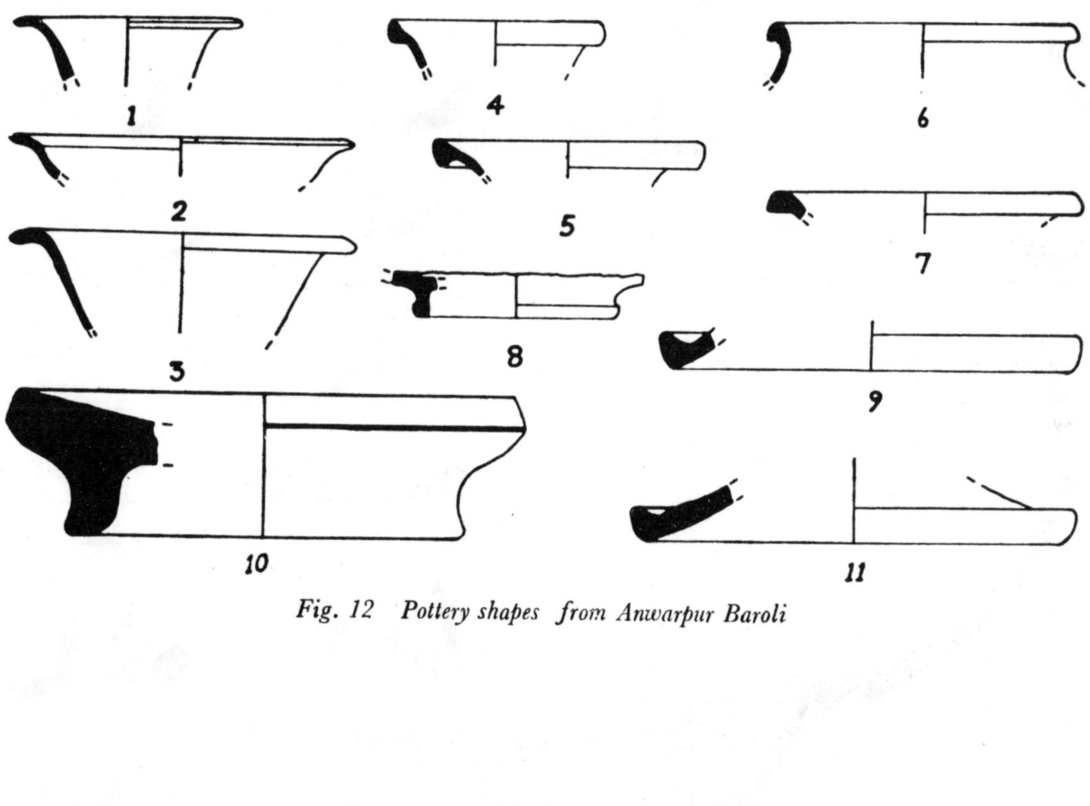

Fig. 12 Pottery shapes from Anwarpur Baroli

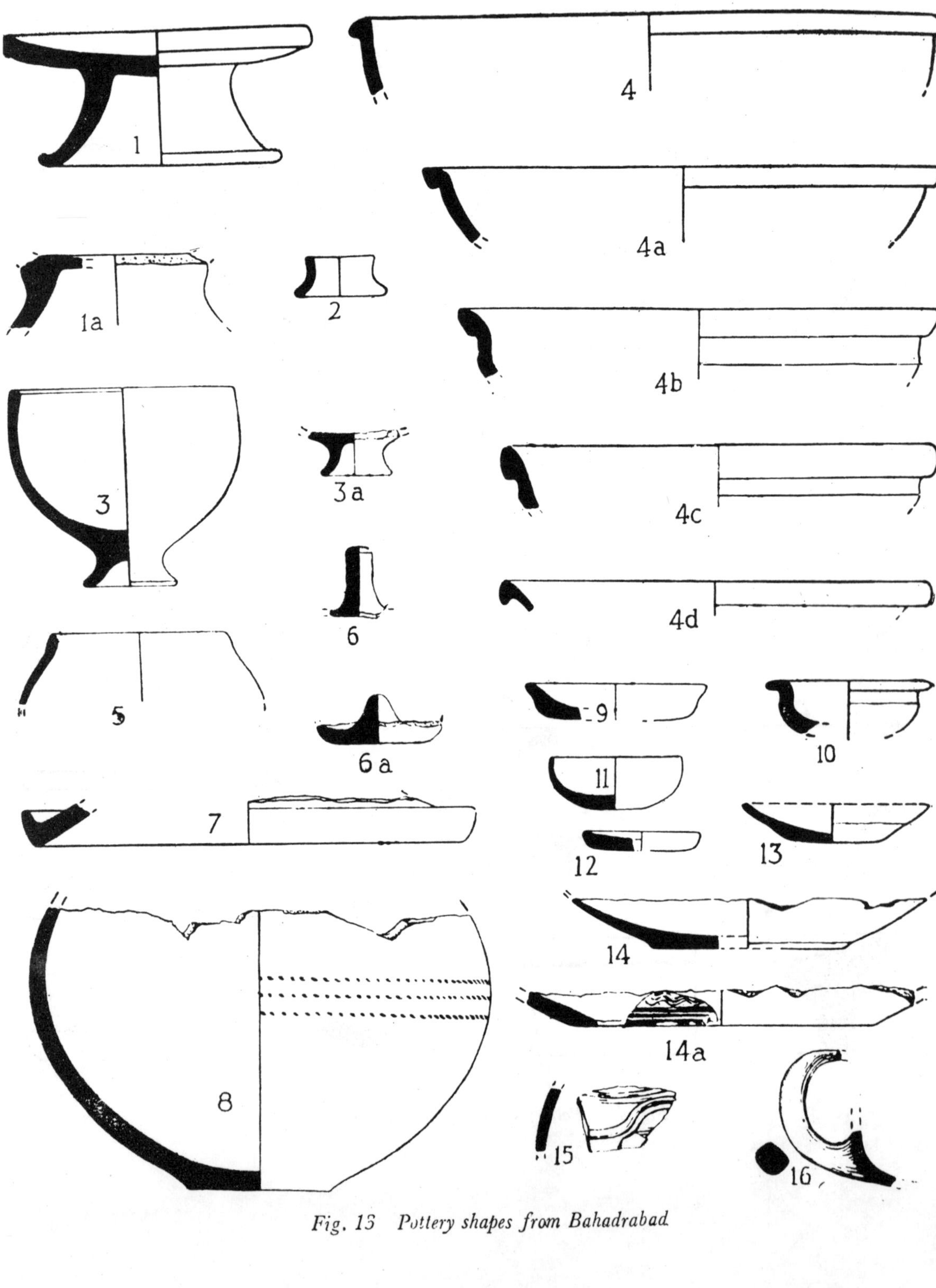

Fig. 13 Pottery shapes from Bahadrabad

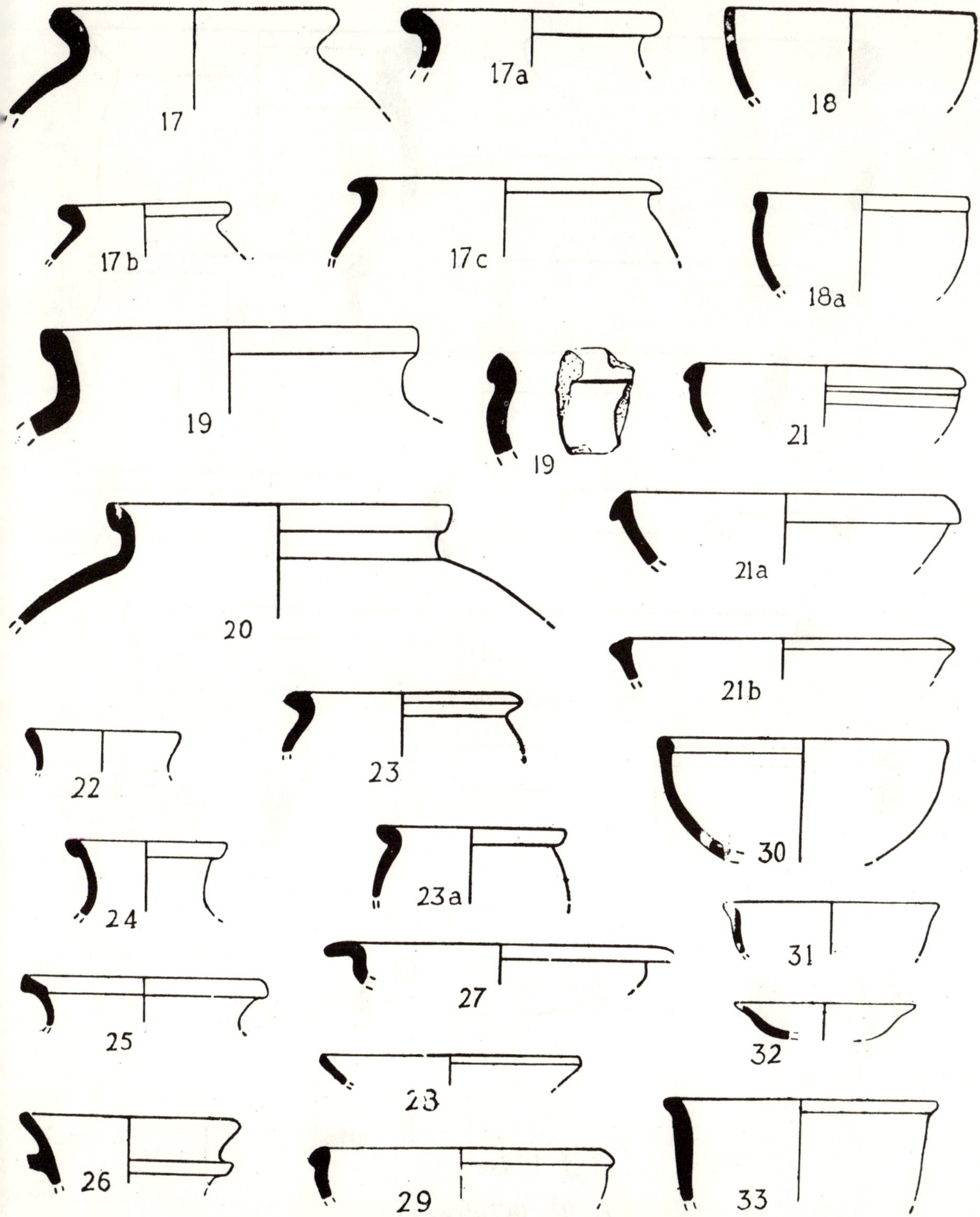

Fig. 14 Pottery shapes from Bahadrabad

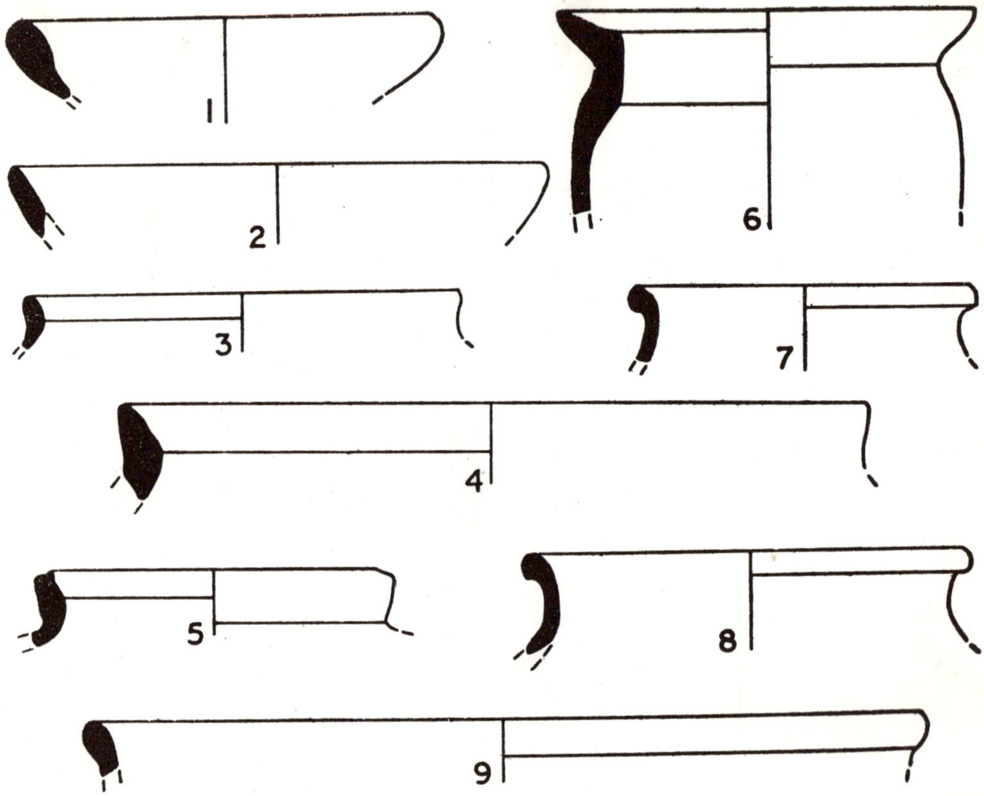

Fig. 16 Pottery shapes from Baharia

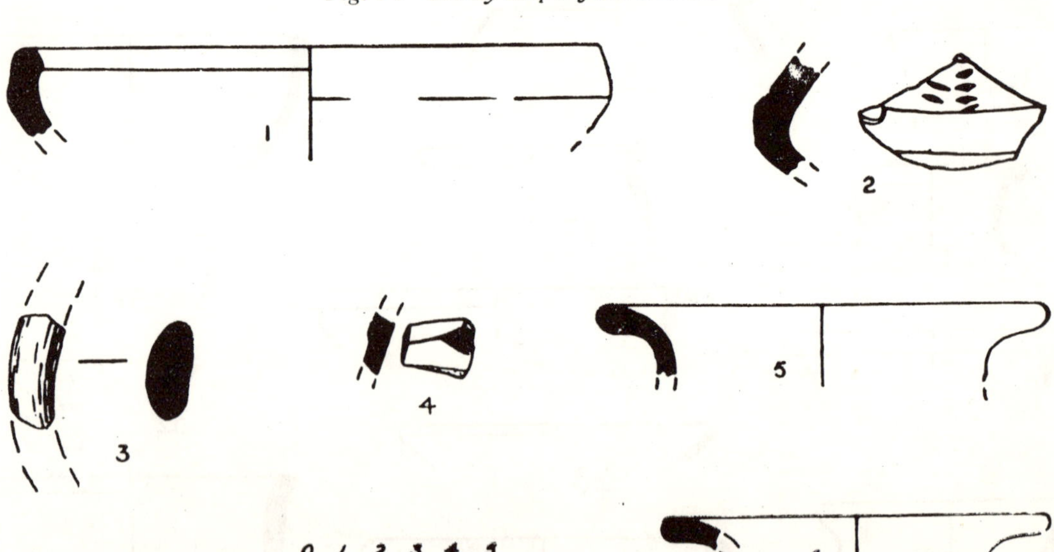

Fig. 17 OCP shapes from Noh

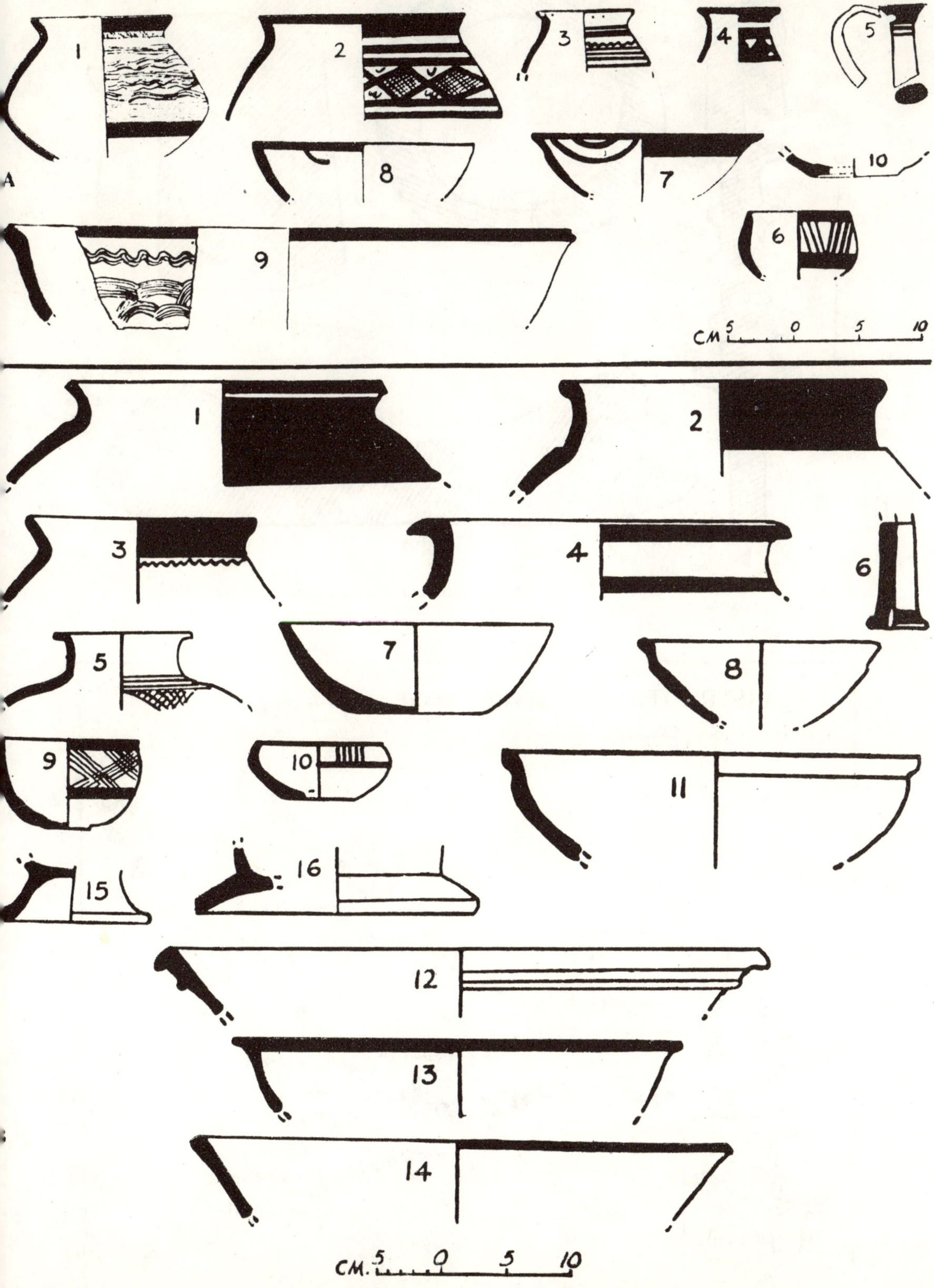

Fig. 18 Pottery from Siswal, Phases A and B

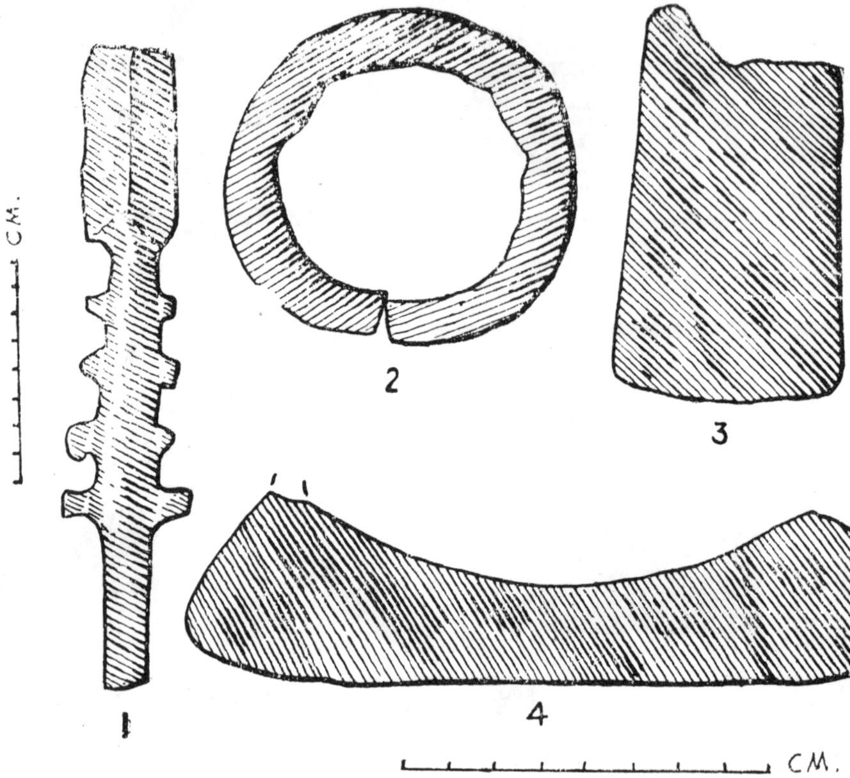

Fig. 19 Copper implements from Mitahal

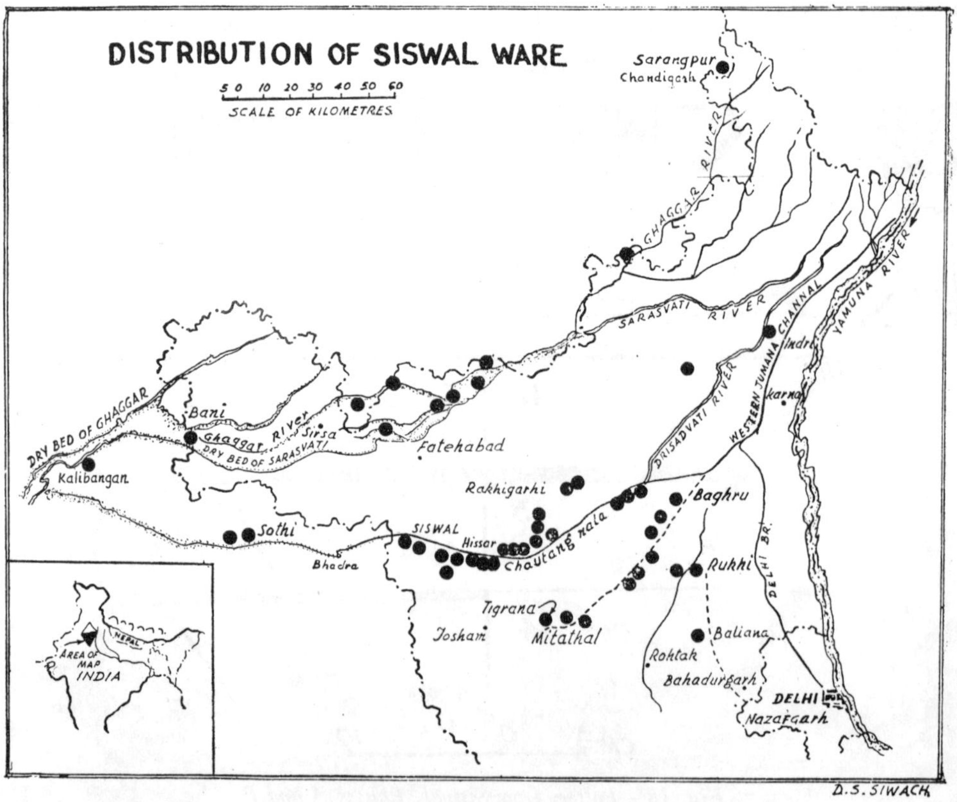

Fig. 20 Distribution of Siswal ware

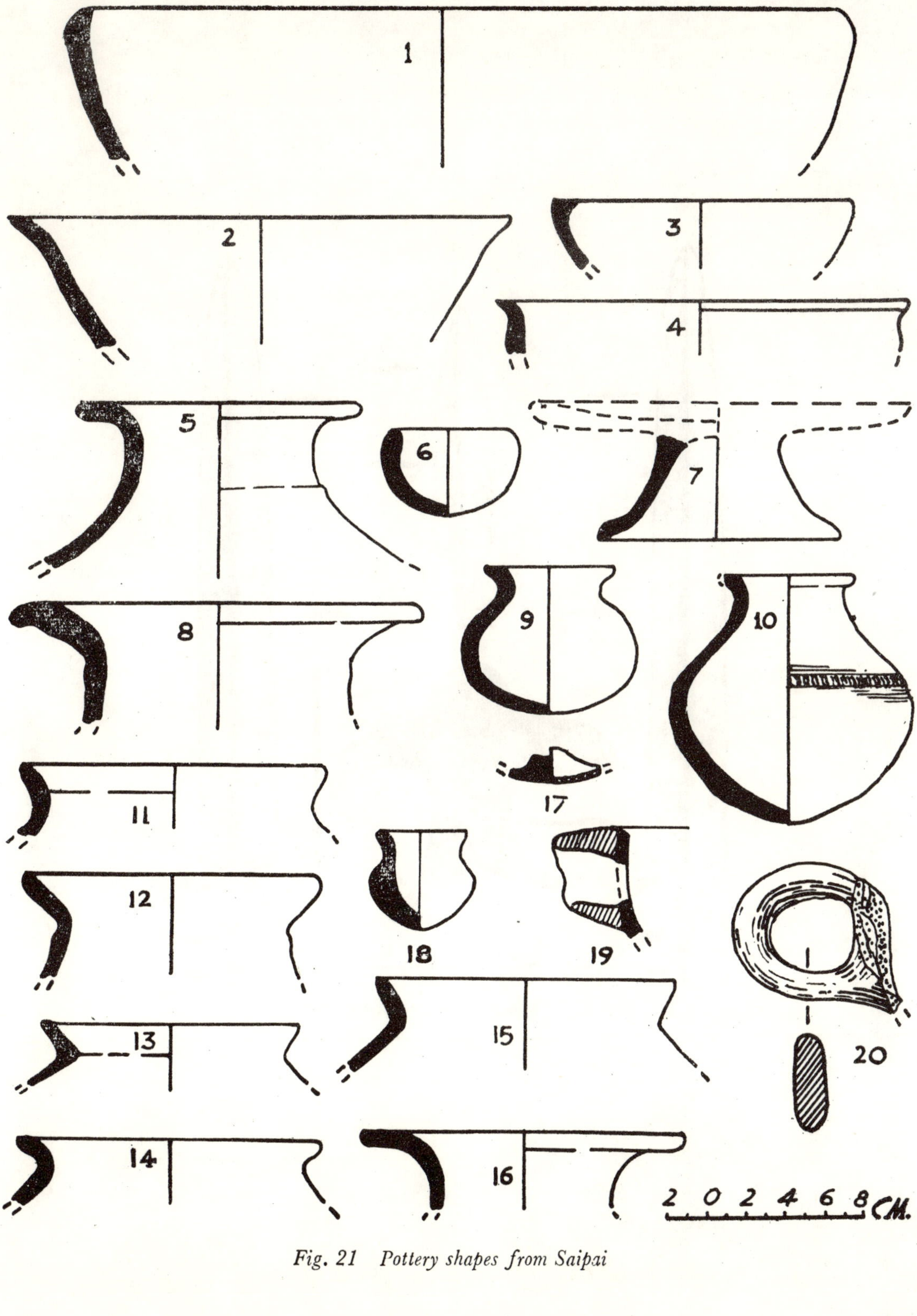

Fig. 21 Pottery shapes from Saipai

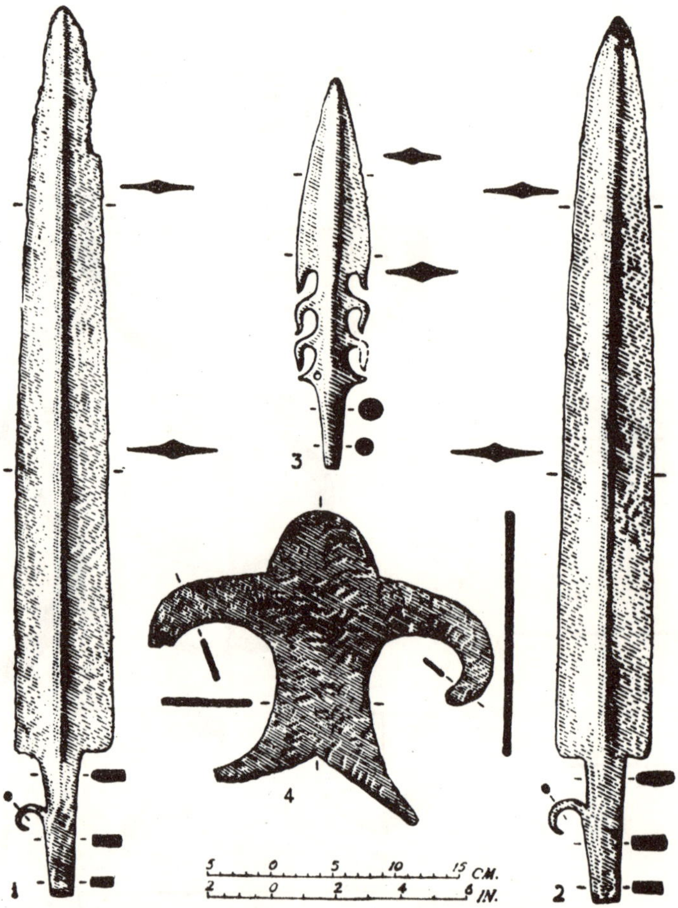

Fig. 22 Copper implements from Saipai.

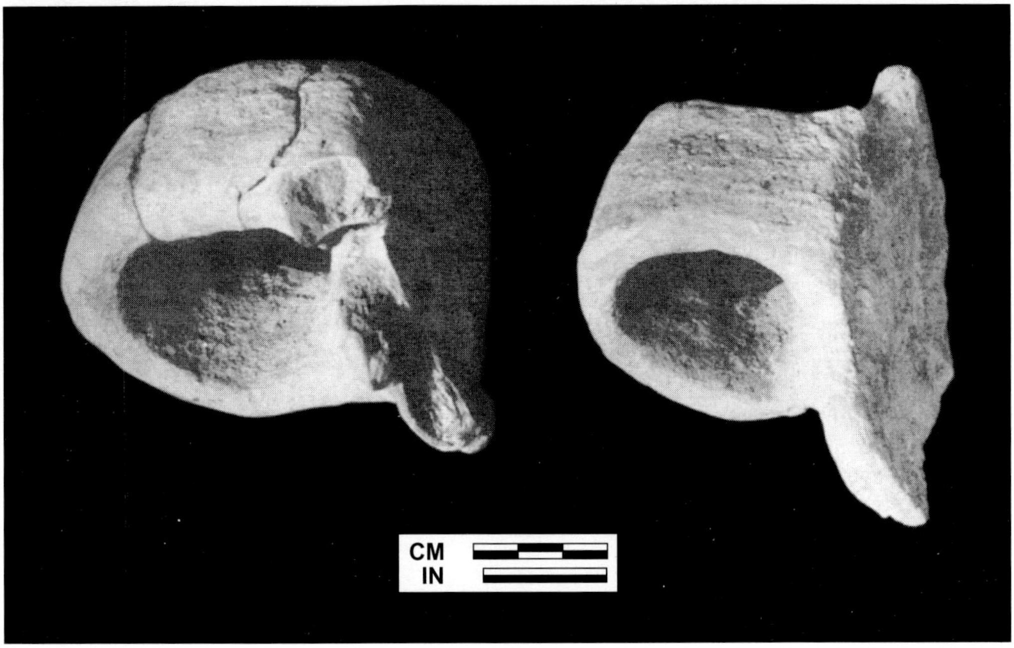

A. Saipai : handles of pottery.

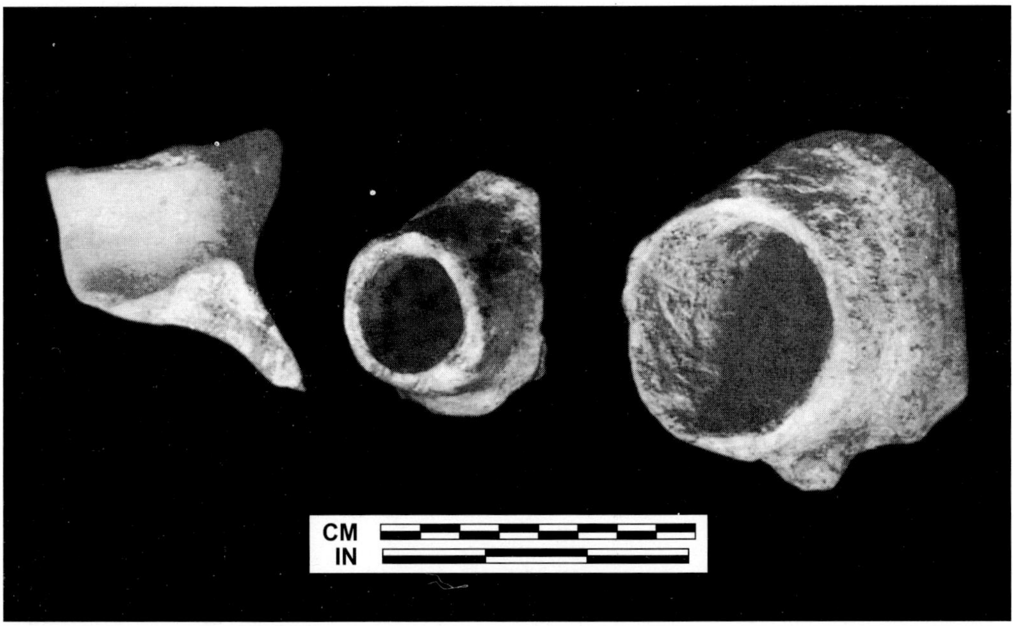

B. Saipai : spouts of pottery.

A. Copper implements from Baharia.

B. Saipai : Copper harpoon *in situ* during excavation.

READINGS IN INDIAN ARCHAEOLOGY

(Abstracts from "A Deluge ? Which Deluge ? Yet Another Facet of Problem of the Copper Hoard Culture" by B. B. Lal, published in *American Anthropologist*, Vol. 70, 1968, pp. 857-863. One figure and two plates.)

The purpose of the present paper is to place before archaeologists and allied workers an altogether different aspect of the problem. At Hastinapura (Lal, 1954 & 1955 :10–11) the sherds of Ocher Color Ware found in a very hard deposit of brown earth. In this deposit there was no ash, no flooring, nor any of the other signs one usually comes across in a regular habitational stratum. The frequency, too, of the sherds was very limited. One stroke of the big pickaxe might turn up not more than a couple of sherds; in fact, often there was none. The sherds occurred sporadically to a depth of about half a meter in the brown earth, which continued downward, merging imperceptibly into the natural soil. It was also observed that the upper part, 10-15 cm. in thickness, of the brown earth was darker than that below it, which might indicate that the top of this deposit remained exposed for a long time before the site was occupied by the succeeding Painted Gray Ware people.

At Bahadrabad (Krishnaswami, 1953 : 71) the copper objects as well as the pottery came from a deposit that lay about 6 meters below the general ground level—with no mound formation whatsoever. This overlying deposit consisted of sand, pebbles, and earth. The stratum that yielded the pottery and the copper hoard was about a meter in thickness and consisted of hard brownish earth. Available accounts show that there was no floor level or any similar sign indicative of a regular occupation.

Several years ago copper objects had been recovered from Nasirpur—celts, a harpoon, a hooked spearhead, etc.—which are now lodged at the Gurukul Kangri University Museum, near Hardwar. A recent examination of the locality showed that there was no habitational layer as such, but the natural looking, yellowish brown earth did contain sherds that, on the basis of their color and texture, may be regarded as belonging to the same general family of the so-called Ocher Color Ware. The sherds were found to occur sporadically and down to a depth of about 1½ meters below the general ground-level.

Jhinjhana has not so far yielded any copper object, but the section at this site is quite important. As at Hastinapura, so also here, the deposit bearing the Ocher Color Ware underlay the one yielding Painted Gray Ware, and the two stood in marked contrast to each other. Thus, while the Painted Gray Ware came from regular occupational layers with floors and habitational debris, including ash, charcoal, etc.

the Ocher Color Ware occurred in a deposit of brown earth devoid of any ash charcoal, or floor-material The sherds, too, did not lie in an orderly fashion, forming for example, a layer, but occurred sporadically. In this manner they went down to a depth of about one and a quarter meters. The soil itself showed some interesting features. The uppermost 10-15 cm. strip was dark in color. An examination of it was clearly called for, as it might reveal humic contents, suggesting that the top remained exposed for quite some time before the arrival of the Painted Gray Ware people. The next lower strip, about 30 cm. in thickness, was lighter in color than the ones above or below it. Maybe it was leached in the course of time—a guess that is being checked through a chemical examination. Lastly, there was no hard and fast demarcation between the soil yielding the pottery and the one below it, although lower down *kankars* (nodules of calcium carbonate) began to make their appearance.

At Gadharona, the sherds of the Ocher Color Ware were picked up very near the surface, from a matrix of sand and silt. However, as the site seems to have undergone subsequent disturbance, it is difficult to say whether the sherds lay in their original matrix or whether they had been displaced and subsequently re-embedded in the present deposit.

The story at Achichchhatra is similar to that at Hastinapura and Jhinjhana. Thus, here too, below the Painted Gray ware strata lay a hard brown earth in which sherds of the Ocher Color Ware occurred sporadically, up to a depth of about 60 cm. (Government of India 1964/65). This deposit continued even lower, though without the sherds. All through, the brown earth did not contain any ash, charcoal, or other material indicative of a regular habitation.

At Atranji khera the Painted Gray Ware strata were underlain by a 15 to 40 cm. deposit containing Black-and-Red Ware, and it was below this that the Ocher Color Ware occurred (Government of India 1963/64:45-47). The deposit yielding the last-named pottery varied from 0·8 to 1·5 meters in thickness and consisted of yellowish brown earth mixed with *Kankar*. There were no signs of any regular habitation.

The sequence at Noh (Government of India 1964/65) is identical with that at Atranjikhera, for here too the Black-and-Red Ware intervened between the Painted Gray and Ocher Color Wares. The sherds of the last-named ware lay sparsely in a matrix of brownish earth that merged into the natural soil. The deposit was devoid of ash, charcoal, floor material, etc.

The preceding account presents a more or less uniform picture from all the sites, namely that the Ocher Color Ware occurred in a deposit of earth, varying from yellowish brown to dark brown in color, often mixed with *kankar* and usually hard in texture, which did not contain any flooring substance or ash or charcoal or for that matter any other object indicative of the layer having been a regular habitational one. If this be so, a query arises as to how the earth came to be deposited and how the sherds found their way into it. The absence of habitational symptoms precludes human agency, unless it is argued that the earth was rammed down by human beings for some purpose and that the sherds came in along with it. This might seem to be all right theoretically, but sounds somewhat unrealistic, particularly when the same pattern is repeated at so many sites, located far away from one another. Thus, one has to look for some other explanation. At the moment, the following possibilities suggest themselves. There could, obviously, be many more.

The simplest explanation would be that the soil, a naturally laid one, developed fissures, like those occurring in the black cotton-soil of central India and the Deccan, and that the sherds, which had been lying about on the ground, found their way into it through the fissures. Such an explanation, however, would involve at least two assumptions, namely that (1) this soil is capable of developing fissures, and even very deep fissures, for the sherds have been found down to a depth of about $1\frac{1}{2}$ meters from the top, and (2) there was some settlement in the neighborhood, the inhabitants of which left the sherds on the surface, say while ploughing the field or in some other way. On the first assumption the present writer is not competent to comment. All that he can say is that he has not seen this soil develop such fissures—maybe its sand content prevents it from so doing. The second assumption requires the existence, in each case, of a regular settlement of the Ocher Color Ware people somewhere in the neighborhood. As in this hypothesis the settlement site is not thought to have been affected in any way, it should still be available. The writer, however, has come across no such site.

If the above is not the likely explanation, what else would be ? At my request, Dr. B. B. Lal, Chief Archaeological Chemist, Archaeological Survery of India, and his colleagues have undertaken a detailed study of soil samples from Hastinapura, Jhinjhana, Ahichchhatra, Nasirpur and Atranji khera. Their preliminary investigations suggest that the deposits may have been water laid. Professor Fakhruddin Ahmad, Head of the Department of Geology, Aligarh Muslim University, and his colleagues, who independently examined the soil samples from Atranjikhera are, according to the excavators, of the view that "the area had been flooded by the river and remained waterlogged for a considerable period, which may explain the absence of the usual habitation marks" (Gaur & Hasan 1964: 5—6).

Now, if a flood is to be invoked to explain the nature of the deposit at Atranjikhera, the same will have to be done in the case of the rest of the sites. This would involve the flooding of almost the whole of the upper basin of the Ganga, Yamuna and their tributaries. From Bahadrabad in the north to Noh in the south is a distance of about 300 km., and from the longitude of Jhinjhana in the west to that of Ahichchhatra in the east measures about 200 km. And if, on examination, similar deposits are found at the copper hoard sites further downstream, the flood will have to be nothing less than a "deluge."

Assuming for a moment that this turns out to be the case, one would naturally look for the causes of the deluge. Among various possibilities the following three may have to be considered.

(1) Incessant rain for a sufficiently long period might cause sheet flooding of the entire basin, because of the limited draining capacity of the plain and also of the rivers, which do not have a steep gradient. In such an event the settlements would be submerged, and while the lighter material, like ash, charcoal, etc, would float away, heavier articles like pottery, "copper hoards" and the like, would no doubt get mixed up with the muddy soil but would resettle in more or less the same area, without being carried far away.

(2) The flooding of the Upper Ganga Yamuna basin could also have occurred if, through some tectonic movement, a barrier was created across the river system somewhere lower down, such as, for example, has been postulated by Raikes (1965) for the flooding of the lower Indus basin, involving Mohenjo-daro. If it were a barrier of earth, it would soon be broken through by the waters and the deluge would be short-lived, but long enough to produce the kind of pottery-mixed strata referred to above. Or, a less drastic explanation might be that local tectonic movements led to widespread changes in the courses of the Ganga, Yamuna and their upper tributaries, resulting in widespread flooding

(3) In a third possibility, one has to imagine a tectonic movement involving the divide between the Indus and Ganga systems, say somewhere near the source, where the Ghaggar and Yamuna basins come close to each other (Fig.1). Such a possibility comes to mind because we must also account for the drying up of the Ghaggar, which could have resulted from the diversion of some of its tributaries to a neighboring system, in this case that of the Yamuna. In this context it may not be out of place to mention two points. First, if the desertion of the Harappan site of Kalibangan is to be attributed to the drying up of the Ghaggar, as is not altogether unlikely, the latter event would have to be placed broadly in the first half of the second millennium B.C. (Lal 1962 & 1963: 212, 219). Secondly, the occurrence of the anthropomorphic figure, even though fragmentary, in the late levels of Phase IV at Lothal shows that the copper hoard culture was in existence in the first quarter of the second millennium B.C. (Lal (1962 & 1963: 220). Thus, at least from the chronological point of view an interrelation between the drying up of the Ghaggar and the flooding of the copper hoard sites may not be altogether incompatible.

BOOK REVIEWS

INDIA'S CONTRIBUTION TO WORLD THOUGHT AND CULTURE

Vivekananda Commemoration Volume (Editors : Lokesh Chandra, S.P. Gupta, Sitaram Goel and Devendra Swarup), Vivekananda Rock Memorial Committee, 12 Pillaiyar Koil Street, Triplicane, Madras-5, 705+XVI+lii pp., 200 half-tone and 19 colour plates besides numerous line-drawings. Price : Rs. 150.00.

A comprehensive volume dealing with the various facets of India's contribution to world thought and culture and incorporating the results of the latest researches, has been a desideratum. The publication of a volume on the occasion of the inauguration of the Vivekananda Rock Memorial at Kanyakumari, in September 1970, fulfills this long-felt need.

Dealing as this does with the history of Indian culture in general and its proselytizing influence in foreign countries, the Volume contains articles which primarily describe those geographical areas and periods about which tangible evidence is available in the form of monumental remains and literary traditions. In fact, a majority of articles deal with India's cultural influence as manifested in the art, architecture, religion, literature, etc., of foreign countries, both in the adjoining and remotely situated areas which are bound together by common cultural heritage.

The range of articles in the Volume is very comprehensive. Thus, while we have papers like 'Red Indians or Asioamericans: Indian Settlers in Middle and South America' (D. P. Singhal), 'India's Contacts with Africa from the Earliest Times' (Amba Prasad) and 'Indian Culture in Transbaikalian Siberia' (Lokesh Chandra), which give us an idea of India's relationship with these distant lands, there are certain papers which give an entirely new perspective, e.g., Jose Pereira's 'The Plan of the Hindu Temple and its Impact on the Baroque Church'. Likewise, the various aspects of cultural relationship with the lands nearer India have also been covered. Particular interest attaches to the very learned analyses in J. Gonda's article 'The Presence of Hinduism in Indonesia : Aspects and Problems', Ludwik Sternbach's 'Sanskrit Niti-Literature in "Greater India"', and Pentti Aalto's 'On the Role of Central Asia in the Spread of Indian Cultural Influence'. To those unacquainted with the achievements of Indians in the field of physical sciences and medicine, B.V. Subbarayappa's 'India's Contributions to the History of Science', Jean Filliozat's 'The Expansion of Indian Medicine Abroad', Arjun Dev's 'India in the Eyes of Early Muslim Scholars' and W. H. Siddiqui's 'India's Contribution to the Arab Civilization' should give an inkling into this important aspect of India's glorious achievements in the past.

The movements of peoples and thereby of the ideas depend *ipso facto* upon the mobility which is proved by trade and maritime activity. S. R. Rao's 'Shipping in Ancient India,' K. S. Ramachandran's 'Ancient Indian Maritime Ventures' and Lallanji Gopal's 'Indian Shipping in the Mediaeval Period' are of value for those interested in this aspect even though there is duplication and, in a few cases necessary corroborative details have not been given by the authors.

Apart from these, there are articles of a different genre which have been included in the Volume which seek to analyze the course of Indian history. M. C. Joshi's 'Self-Renewal in Indian History and Swami Vivekananda' is an analysis of the factors which have provided substance and sustenance to the people of India and because of which they have been able to keep alive and intact the innate traditions despite the many setbacks they were faced with. N. C. Ghosh has shown in his paper 'The Impact of Indian Tradition on the Coins of the Alien Rulers of India,' the capacity for absorption and the almost charismatic quality of Indian culture which was imbibed even by the alien rulers of India.

It may not be out of place to mention here also the contribution of the Western Indologists towards the study of Indian history, culture and civilization. Nevertheless, some of their writings, which have added many a new chapter in the history of India, were not free from bias of one kind or the other. Kailash Chandra Varma, in his paper 'Some Western Indologists and Indian Civilization', has analyzed the writings of these pioneer scholars, some of which 'were vitiated by political or religious or theological bias' as a result of which there has been, at times, 'gross misrepresentation of India and the Indians, particularly the Hindus, in the Western world and specially in the English-speaking world and the United States of America.' It comes as surprise that even scholars of high calibre like H. H. Wilson and Max Mueller were not free from such bias. Varma's article is a pointer to those who rely solely upon these writings without critically examining them. In fact, there is an urgent need for re-evaluating their writings and, if necessery to re-write the history of India, without, however, succumbing to the narrow and partisan chauvinistic sentiments which are now characteristic of the writings of the Indians belonging to either a particular region or a linguistic group or creed.

In this review it is not possible to evaluate all the articles which deal with varied subjects and areas. It must, however, be added that the attempt to combine the results of latest archaeological researches with the historical studies is a commendable feature of this Volume. This has to be stated for, more often than not, in most of the writings of the Indian historians the archaeological data are not properly included.

Those engaged in digging India's past would be particularly interested in the articles dealing with those periods or subjects which, in the current archaeological jargon, come under the purview of the pre- and protohistoric periods and about which traditions—written or oral—are non-existent and are highly debatable in nature. It, therefore, goes to the credit of the editors of the Volume to have included papers, which although deviate from the main theme, have relevence to the subject.

The Aryan problem and the decipherment of the Harappan script are two such issues which, despite the many hypotheses and theories, still remain undecided or are highly controversial. B. K. Thapar's article on the Aryan problem not only deals with the various theories about their original homeland, but also establishes the point that 'the archaeological and anthropological evidences, represented by the various culture-groups of the second millennium B.C. are inconsistent with the philological evidence, and that *the available objective evidence for the movement of Aryans into India is still inconclusive*' (author's emphasis).

B. B. Lal has reviewed in his article the 'decipherments' of the Harappan script by scholars in the years immediately preceding the publication of the present Volume and has tried to prove conclusively that the direction of writing in the Harappan script was from right to left. While he has discussed the 'decipherments' by the Finns, Krishna Rao and Fateh Singh, he has omitted the equally important and interesting work of the Soviet scholars on the subject. This, along with his own views on the problem, would have been welcome to the readers.

Much new information is given by S. P. Gupta in his paper 'Prehistoric Indian Cultures in Soviet Central Asia' wherein he has tried to show 'that the dispersal of Indian cultures, at least in Soviet Central Asia, can be traced back to the earliest times, i.e., to the Early Stone Age.' This, according to him, takes back the history of India's contact to about half a million years on the basis of 'well-established archaeological evidence in the Soviet Republics of Tajikistan, Uzbekistan, Turkmenia and Kazakhstan.' While the similarities in the shape of tools found in the Soviet Central Asia no duobt led a Soviet scholar in calling the Borykazghan assemblage as "the Soan Cultura of Central Asia", one would rather agree with what Prof. R. C. Majumdar has stated in his Foreword to the Volume that 'such studies of cultural contact between primitive peoples, being based solely on stone tools or other artefacts, can only give us very meagre and vague ideas on the subject of what we properly recongnise as human culture.' Much more tangible are the data pertaining to the contacts between the two regions in the Bronze Age in the third millennium B.C., which extend the limits of the Harappan Culture into the hitherto unknown areas.

This compendium on Indian culture is one of the best-produced books on the subject and should find a place in the libraries as a most sought-after book. For the lay reader it should serve as an 'appetizer' and stimulating his interest for knowing more about India's glorious past.

B. M. Pande

GLIMPSES OF NEPAL WOODWORK

(published by the Indian Society of Oriental Art, New Series, vol. III, Calcutta, 1968-69,) pp. 48 and 38 plates, price Rs. 25/-

by S. B. Deo

The book under review is the third volume of the Journal of Indian Society of Oriental Art, Calcutta. After Dr. Stella Kramrisch's well-known work *The Art of Nepal* this is a rich contribution to the Art History of Nepal. The author has skilfully dealt with the various characteristics of Nepal woodwork of the 17th-19th centuries. No architectural monument built earlier than the fifteenth century seems to have survived to this date.

Nepal, located as it is in the Himalayan abode, has had very intimate contacts with India, running through several centuries, although the flow of Tibetan elements in Nepal has not been less significant. In the field of art, however, the impact of Indian cultural traditions has been more pronounced. The author has presented some of the most representative and significant specimens of the art of woodwork at Patan, Kathmandu and Bhadgaon. The data that has been collected relates to three classes of structures, viz., the temples, the viharas, and the residential palaces and towers. The architectural peculiarities of wooden structures of Nepal comprise the use of heavy wooden framework, ingenious arrangement of load distribution with the help of structs and bracket capitals projecting window groups, multi-storeyed receding roofs, massive pillars and elaborate window and door-frames. All these were due to the meticulous technique adopted by the Newari artisans whose origin and antiquity is still a matter of controversy. That they could execute their skill with rather limited tools is indeed remarkable. While reconstructing the history of that art Deo has furnished all the technical details of the different members of the scheme of architecture, together with the decorative motifs such as the tympanum, the wall band, the cave board and the erotic scenes. Finally, the author has referred to the influence of south India on the history and architecture of Nepal—for instance, the Mallas who were proud of tracing their descent from Karnataka, invited pandits from Maharashtra. As for the architecture, the author has cited certain parallels from Indian counterparts—the Chalukyan bands of delicately chiselled fretwork, perforated stone-grills with diaper pattern, the square mesh with floral decoration, etc. Even in the domain of religious-motifs, the *purna-kalasa, naga-nagis, Ganga and Yamuna*, the *Kala-makara*, the *vyalas*, the *vidyadharas*, are all reminiscent of their counterparts in Indian architecture. Inspite of all these good features, the treatment of the subject is rather sketchy.

The book has been nicely printed with beautiful plates and a map of the Kathmandu valley.

Krishna Deva